SkillBuilder

Grade 7

English Workbook - 1

▸ *Reading: Literature*
▸ *Reading: Informational Text*

Complement Classroom Learning All Year

Using the Lumos Study Program, parents and teachers can reinforce the classroom learning experience for children. It creates a collaborative learning platform for students, teachers and parents.

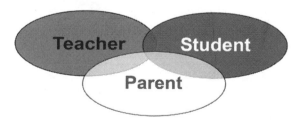

Used in Schools and Libraries To Improve Student Achievement

Lumos Learning
Developed by Expert Teachers

Contributing Editor   - Stacy Zeiger
Contributing Editor   - Mechelle Craig
Contributing Author   - Marisa Adams
Executive Producer   - Mukunda Krishnaswamy
Designer and Illustrator - Sowmya R.

ISBN-10: 1-940484-95-2

ISBN-13: 978-1-940484-95-2

Printed in the United States of America

For permissions and additional information contact us

Lumos Information Services, LLC
Email: support@lumoslearning.com

PO Box 1575
Piscataway, NJ 08855-1575
Tel: (732) 384-0146
Fax: (866) 283-6471

http://www.LumosLearning.com

Developed by Expert Teachers

Lumos Reading Comprehension Skill Builder, Grade 7 - Literature, Informational Text and Evidence-based Reading

This Book Includes:

- Practice questions to help students master
  ‣ Reading: Literature
  ‣ Reading: Informational Text
- Detailed Answer explanations for every question
- Strategies for building speed and accuracy

Plus access to Online Workbooks which include:

- Instructional videos
- Mobile apps related to the learning objective
- Hundreds of additional practice questions
- Self-paced learning and personalized score reports
- Instant feedback after completion of the workbook

Table of Contents

Introduction

Books in the Lumos Skill Builder series are designed to help students master specific skills in Math and English Language Arts. The content of each workbook is rigorous and aligned with the robust standards. Each standard, and substandard, has its own specific content. Taking the time to study and practice each standard individually can help students more adequately understand and demonstrate proficiency of that standard in their particular grade level.

Unlike traditional printed books, this book provides online access to engaging educational videos, mobile apps and assessments. Blending printed resources with technology based learning tools and resources has proven to be an effective strategy to help students of the current generation master learning objectives. We call these books tedBooks™ since they connect printed books to a repository of online learning resources!

Additionally, students have individual strengths and weaknesses. Being able to practice content by standard allows them the ability to more deeply understand each standard and be able to work to strengthen academic weaknesses. The online resources create personalized learning opportunities for each student and provides immediate individualized feedback.

We believe that yearlong learning and adequate practice before the test are the keys to success on standardized tests. The books in the Skill Builder series will help students gain foundational skills needed to perform well on the standardized tests.

How to Use this Book Effectively

The Lumos Program is a flexible learning tool. It can be adapted to suit a student's skill level and the time available to practice. Here are some tips to help you use this book and the online resources effectively:

Students

- The standards in each book can be practiced in the order designed, or in the order of your own choosing.
- Answer all questions in each workbook.
- Use the online workbooks to further practice your areas of difficulty and complement classroom learning.
- Watch videos recommended for the lesson or question.
- Download and try mobile apps related to what you are learning.

Parents

- Get student reports and useful information about your school by downloading the Lumos SchoolUp™ app. Please follow directions provided in "How to download Lumos SchoolUp™ App" section of this chapter.
- Review your child's performance in the "Lumos Online Workbooks" periodically. You can do this by simply asking your child to log into the system online and selecting the subject area you wish to review.
- Review your child's work in each workbook.

- You can use the Lumos online programs along with this book to complement and extend your classroom instruction.
- Get a Free Teacher account by visiting http://lumoslearning.com/a/fta

This Lumos StepUp® Basic account will help you:

- Create up to 30 student accounts.
- Review the online work of your students.
- Create and share information about your classroom or school events.

NOTE: There is a limit of one grade and subject per teacher for the free account.

- Download the Lumos SchoolUp™ mobile app using the instructions provided in "How can I Download the App?" section of this chapter to conveniently monitor your students online progress.

How to Access the Lumos Online Workbooks

First Time Access:

Using a personal computer with internet access:	Using a smartphone or tablet:
Go to http://www.lumoslearning.com/a/workbooks	Scan the QR Code below and follow the instructions.
Select your State and enter the following access code in the Access Code field and press the Submit button.	
Access Code: NCG7LR-17380-P	

In the next screen, click on the "Register" button to register your username and password.

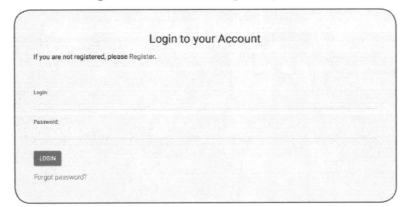

Subsequent Access:

After you establish your user id and password for subsequent access, simply login with your account information.

What if I buy more than one Lumos Study Program?

Please note that you can use all Online Workbooks with one User ID and Password. If you buy more than one book, you will access them with the same account.

Go back to the **http://lumoslearning.com/a/workbooks** link and enter the access code provided in the second book. In the next screen simply login using your previously created account.

Lumos StepUp® Mobile App FAQ For Students

What is the Lumos StepUp® App?

It is a FREE application you can download onto your Android smart phones, tablets, iPhones, and iPads.

What are the Benefits of the StepUp® App?

This mobile application gives convenient access to Practice Tests, Common Core State Standards, On-line Workbooks, and learning resources through your smart phone and tablet computers.

- Eleven Technology enhanced question types in both MATH and ELA
- Sample questions for Arithmetic drills
- Standard specific sample questions
- Instant access to the Common Core State Standards
- Jokes and cartoons to make learning fun!

Do I Need the StepUp® App to Access Online Workbooks?

No, you can access Lumos StepUp® Online Workbooks through a personal computer. The StepUp® app simply enhances your learning experience and allows you to conveniently access StepUp® Online Workbooks and additional resources through your smart phone or tablet.

How can I Download the App?

Visit **lumoslearning.com/a/stepup-app** using your smart phone or tablet and follow the instructions to download the app.

**QR Code
for Smart Phone
Or Tablet Users**

Lumos SchoolUp™ Mobile App FAQ For Parents and Teachers

What is the Lumos SchoolUp™ App?

It is a free app that teachers can use to easily access real-time student activity information as well as assign learning resources to students. Parents can also use it to easily access school-related information such as homework assigned by teachers and PTA meetings. It can be downloaded onto smart phones and tablets from popular App Stores.

What are the Benefits of the Lumos SchoolUp™ App?

It provides convenient access to
- Real-time student activity information.
- School "Stickies". A Sticky could be information about an upcoming test, homework, extra curricular activities and other school events. Parents and educators can easily create their own sticky and share with the school community.
- Discover useful educational videos and mobile apps.
- Common Core State Standards.
- Educational blogs.
- StepUp™ student activity reports.

How can I Download the App?

Visit **lumoslearning.com/a/schoolup-app** using your smartphone or tablet and follow the instructions provided to download the App. Alternatively, scan the QR Code provided below using your smartphone or tablet computer.

**QR Code
for Smart Phone
Or Tablet Users**

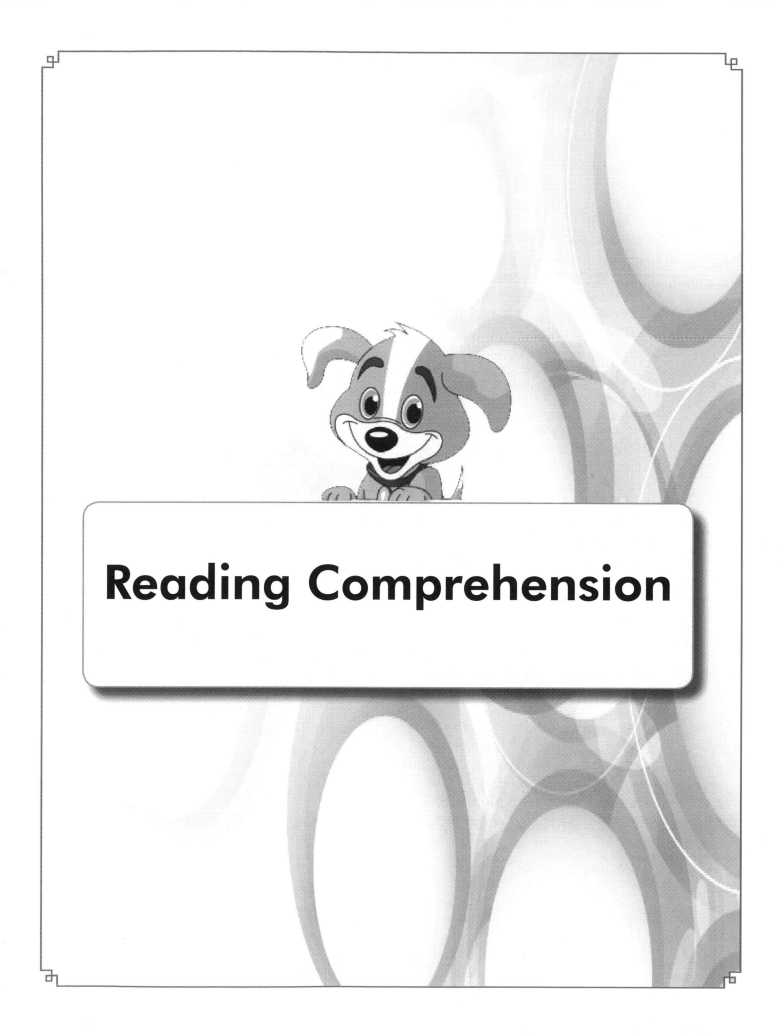

Reading Comprehension

From *Scouting for Boys*

"Hi! Stop Thief!" shouted old Blenkinsopp as he rushed out of his little store near the Kaffir village. "He's stolen my sugar. Stop him."

Stop whom? There was nobody in sight running away, "Who stole it?" asked the policeman.

"I don't know, but a whole bag of sugar is missing. It was there only a few minutes ago." A native police tracker was called in and it looked a pretty impossible job for him to single out the tracks of the thief from among dozens of other footprints about the store. However, he presently started off hopeful, at a jog-trot, away out into the bush. In some places he went over hard stony ground, but he never checked his pace, although no foot marks could be seen. People wondered how he could possibly find the trail. Still he trotted on. Old Blenkinsopp was feeling the heat and the pace.

At length the tracker suddenly stopped and cast around having evidently lost the trail. Then a grin came on his face as he pointed with his thumb over his shoulder up the tree near which he was standing. There, concealed among the branches, they saw a native with the missing bag of sugar.

How had the tracker spotted him? His sharp eyes had described some grains of sugar sparkling in the dust. The bag leaked, leaving a slight trail of these grains. He followed that trail and when it came to an end in the bush the tracker noticed a string of ants going up a tree. They were after the sugar, and so was he, and between them they brought about the capture of the thief.

Old Blenkinsopp was so pleased that he promptly opened the bag and spilled a lot of the sugar on the ground as a reward to the ants.

I expect that he also patted the tracker on the back for his cleverness in using his eyes to see the grains of sugar and the ants, and in using his wits to see why the ants were climbing the tree.

1. Why could the policeman not find the footprints from among the others in the shop?

(RL.7.1)

- Ⓐ because they were clearly marked
- Ⓑ there were dozens of footprints
- Ⓒ there were no footprints to be found
- Ⓓ the footprints had been cleaned

2. Who is likely the narrator of this selection? (RL.7.1)

- Ⓐ the shopkeeper
- ● the narrator
- Ⓒ the people
- Ⓓ the thief

3. Based on the details in this story, where can you infer where the story begins (setting)? (RL.7.3)

- Ⓐ a store
- Ⓑ a house
- Ⓒ a bakery
- Ⓓ a police station

4. Why did the old man rush out of the store? (RL.7.3)

- Ⓐ to stop the thief who had stolen his sugar
- Ⓑ to catch the ants
- Ⓒ to go for a walk
- Ⓓ to leave the shop

5. What character, along with the policeman, helped to catch the thief? (RL.7.3)

- Ⓐ the shopkeeper
- Ⓑ the ants
- Ⓒ the villagers
- Ⓓ the shopkeeper's wife

Tryouts

For years, Sam had dreamed of being the best tennis player in the world. He went to tennis practice every single morning, and every single night. He spent every summer at tennis camp, and he gave up long weekends at the beach to work on his game. Now, it seemed his hard work was finally paying off: He was invited to try out for the state tennis team!

Still, there was something that was bothering Sam. The tryouts for the tennis team were on the same day as his mom's birthday, and he knew his family was planning a huge surprise party for her. He didn't want to hurt his mom's feelings by missing the party, but he also didn't want to miss his one shot at being a champion tennis player. He was in a quandary; he didn't know what to do.

For days, Sam went to bed worrying about the decision. If he went to the tryout, he worried he would seem selfish. If he stayed home, he would miss his one big shot at making the state team. In fact, despite the honor of being invited to try out, he hadn't even told his family about the opportunity. He was so stressed about making the decision of whether to go or not that he couldn't even think about sharing the news.

Weeks went by, and Sam was making no progress. Every day his coach asked him if he was ready for the tryout, and Sam couldn't even respond. Finally, Sam couldn't bear the stress any longer. He decided to talk to his grandfather about his predicament.

"You know, your mom wants you to be happy," he told Sam. "It would be a great birthday present for her to know you are making your dream come true."

Sam had never thought of it that way before, and after talking to his grandfather, he knew what he had to do. He immediately went home and sat down with his parents to let them know about the opportunity to try out for the state team. When Sam apologetically told his parents what day the tryouts were, they were so busy shrieking with excitement that he thought maybe they hadn't heard.

"But Mom, that means I'm going to miss your birthday," Sam said. "I am happy you are being so nice about it, but I still feel really bad."

"Are you kidding?" his mom asked? "This is the best present I could ask for!"

1. In this passage, who helps Sam make his choice?   (RL.7.1)

Ⓐ His dog
Ⓑ His neighbor
● His grandfather
Ⓓ His mom

10

2. Which of the following is NOT a sign that Sam's parents raised him well? (RL.7.1)

Ⓐ He understood that family and tennis were both priorities he needed to balance in his life.
Ⓑ He sought guidance from his grandfather instead of running from the problem.
Ⓒ He knew that to become a great tennis player he had to put in a lot of hard work.
Ⓓ Sam didn't care about missing the party.

3. What would be an appropriate alternate title for this story? (RL.7.2)

Ⓐ The Birthday Present
Ⓑ Tennis Trouble
Ⓒ Sam and His Mother
Ⓓ How Sam Ruined His Mother's Birthday

4. What is the theme of the above story? (RL.7.2)

Ⓐ family values and priorities.
Ⓑ pleasing everybody in your family
Ⓒ doing what is very important to you no matter how others feel
Ⓓ sports above all else

5. What message about friendship is this story trying to pass on to readers? (RL.7.2)

Ⓐ Friends can come and go out of each other's lives, but they keep caring about each other.
Ⓑ Friends shouldn't meddle in each other's personal problems.
Ⓒ Friends can often help you see solutions to problems.
Ⓓ You should always ask friends to help you with your life choices.

6. Why was Sam's choice to try out a great birthday present for his mother? (RL.7.3)

Ⓐ She was proud of her son.
Ⓑ She was excited about her birthday.
Ⓒ She loves birthday cake.
Ⓓ She feels younger every day.

7. **What character trait(s) did Sam NOT display in talking to his parents honestly about his tryout and his quandary?** (RL.7.3)

   Ⓐ Integrity – he understood the right thing to do in the situation
   Ⓑ Honesty – he explained why he wanted to go and why he felt bad about it
   Ⓒ Maturity – he was willing to talk to them even though he knew he might not like their answer
   ● Patience - he waited so long to ask for guidance.

8. **Which of the following statements best characterizes Sam?** (RL.7.3)

   Ⓐ Sam is very selfish.
   Ⓑ Sam does not care about what others feel. He just wants to do what he likes.
   Ⓒ Sam is very concerned about others to the point where he would sacrifice his own happiness for someone else's.
   ● Sam can't make decisions easily.

9. **How does Sam's character change as the story progresses?** (RL.7.3)

   Ⓐ Sam goes from being selfish to caring.
   Ⓑ Sam goes from being confident to self-doubting.
   ● Sam goes from being concerned to confident.
   Ⓓ Sam goes from being angry to happy.

Fairy Tales by A Brothers' Grimm

A certain king once fell ill and the doctor declared that only a sudden fright would restore him to health, but the king was not a man for anyone to play tricks on, except his fool.
One day, when the fool was with him in his boat, he cleverly pushed the king into the water. Help had already been arranged and the king was drawn ashore and put to bed. The fright, the bath and the rest in bed cured the diseased king.

The king wanted to frighten the fool for his act so he told him that he would be put to death. He directed the executioner privately not to use the axe but to let fall a single drop of water on the fool's neck. Amidst shouts and laughter, the fool was asked to rise and thank the king for his kindness.
But the fool never move; he was dead; killed by the master's joke.

1. **What trick did the fool plan to cure the king?**   (RL.7.1)

   Ⓐ a lot of medicines
   Ⓑ injections
   ⬤ the sudden push into the water
   Ⓓ the ride in the boat

2. **Based on the relationships between the characters and the plot of this story, who is the only person who can play a trick on the king?**   (RL.7.3)

   Ⓐ the courtiers
   Ⓑ the prince
   ⬤ the fool
   Ⓓ the doctor

3. **How was the king's view of jokes after the fool's death likely different than that of the fool when he was alive?**   (RL.7.3)

   Ⓐ Both had the same view of jokes. Jokes were cruel and unkind.
   ⬤ The fool thought jokes were funny, but the king did not find them amusing.
   Ⓒ The fool realized jokes can sometimes backfire, but the king always thought they would work out in his favor.
   ⬤ The king realized that jokes can sometimes not work out the way you intend for them to play out, but because the fool always had success with his jokes, the king did not consider the fact that his joke might backfire.

"The Boys and the Frogs"
From <u>Aesop's Fables</u>, adapted by Marmaduke Park

Some boys, beside a pond or lake,
Were playing once at duck and drake?
When, doubtless to their heart's content,
Volleys of stones were quickly sent.
But there were some (there will be such)
Who did not seem amused so much;
These were the frogs, to whom the game,
In point of sport was not the same.
For scarce a stone arrived, 'tis said,
But gave some frog a broken head;
And scores in less than half an hour,
Perished beneath the dreadful shower.
At last, said one, "You silly folks, I say,
Do fling your stones another way;
Though sport to you, to throw them thus,
Remember, pray, 'tis death to us!"

100%

1. Why does the frog scold the boys? (RL.7.1)

- Ⓐ The boys hit the frog in the head with a rock.
- Ⓑ The boys are polluting the pond that the frog lives in.
- Ⓒ The boys refuse to let the frog play with them.
- Ⓓ The boys are trying to catch the frog to keep as a pet.

2. According to this poem what are the boys doing at the pond? (RL.7.1)

- Ⓐ Trying to catch fish
- Ⓑ Trying to catch frogs
- Ⓒ Killing frogs
- Ⓓ Throwing stones into the pond *or lake*

3. What is most likely true about the boys in this poem? (RL.7.1)

- Ⓐ They dislike frogs and want to hurt them.
- Ⓑ They did not realize that the rocks would harm the frogs.
- Ⓒ They want to catch the frogs to keep as pets.
- Ⓓ They like rocks more than they like frogs.

14

From "The Dog and the Wolf" by Marmaduke Park

A wolf there was, whose scanty fare
Had made his person lean and spare;
A dog there was, so amply fed,
His sides were plump and sleek; 'tis said
The wolf once met this prosp'rous cur,
And thus began: "Your servant, sir;
I'm pleased to see you look so well,
Though how it is I cannot tell;
I have not broke my fast to-day;
Nor have I, I'm concern'd to say,
One bone in store or expectation,
And that I call a great vexation."

1. Who is speaking in the dialogue of this selection?   (RL.7.1)

Ⓐ The wolf
Ⓑ The dog
Ⓒ The dog's owner
Ⓓ The narrator

2. Which of the following can be inferred about the dog based on this passage? (RL.7.1)

Ⓐ That the dog was a golden retriever
Ⓑ That the dog had a caring master
Ⓒ That the dog was tall
Ⓓ That the dog belonged to the king

3. What does the wolf represent in this poem?

Ⓐ the basic idea of dieting
Ⓑ how to fast (not eat)
Ⓒ the basic needs of living
Ⓓ being a wild animal

4. What does the dog represent in this poem?   (RL.7.1)

Ⓐ being a tamed animal
Ⓑ the comforts of having everything needed in life
Ⓒ being greedy
Ⓓ sharing with others

Jane Eyre (Excerpt)
by Charlotte Bronte

The red-room was a square chamber, very seldom slept in, I might say never, indeed, unless when a chance influx of visitors at Gateshead Hall rendered it necessary to turn to account all the accommodation it contained: yet it was one of the largest and stateliest chambers in the mansion. A bed supported on massive pillars of mahogany, hung with curtains of deep red damask, stood out like a tabernacle in the centre; the two large windows, with their blinds always drawn down, were half shrouded in festoons and falls of similar drapery; the carpet was red; the table at the foot of the bed was covered with a crimson cloth; the walls were a soft fawn colour with a blush of pink in it; the wardrobe, the toilet-table, the chairs were of darkly polished old mahogany. Out of these deep surrounding shades rose high, and glared white, the piled- up mattresses and pillows of the bed, spread with a snowy Marseilles counterpane. Scarcely less prominent was an ample cushioned easy-chair near the head of the bed, also white, with a footstool before it; and looking, as I thought, like a pale throne.

This room was chill, because it seldom had a fire; it was silent, because remote from the nursery and kitchen; solemn, because it was known to be so seldom entered. The house-maid alone came here on Saturdays, to wipe from the mirrors and the furniture a week's quiet dust: and Mrs. Reed herself, at far intervals, visited it to review the contents of a certain secret drawer in the wardrobe, where were stored divers parchments, her jewel-casket, and a miniature of her deceased husband; and in those last words lies the secret of the red-room--the spell which kept it so lonely in spite of its grandeur.

1. Which statement infers the secret of the room?   (RL.7.1)

Ⓐ The room was mainly red because it was haunted.
Ⓑ The lady of the house did not like her rooms to be so dark (furniture and color).
Ⓒ The man of the house (husband) was dead and the room was where he had slept.
Ⓓ The secret is not known to anyone.

2. Why does the author tell us Mrs. Reed only goes there at "far intervals?"   (RL.7.1)

Ⓐ because there is a house-keeper to go in the room
Ⓑ because of the spell cast over the room by her dead husband
Ⓒ because the house if very large and she doesn't go in every room regularly
Ⓓ to explain how busy Mrs. Reed is

3. **Why did the author make a point to say "in spite of its grandeur"?**   (RL.7.1)

- Ⓐ Mrs. Reed's husband asked her to leave the room like it was when he lived.
- Ⓑ Mrs. Reed does not want to dirty the room after the maid has cleaned.
- Ⓒ The room is too pretty to use, so Mrs. Reed only goes there occasionally.
- Ⓓ The author is saying that the room was so pretty that people would normally want to spend time there, but not Mrs. Reed.

4. **Which sentence best summarizes the description of this room?**   (RL.7.2)

- Ⓐ It was a cold, quiet room.
- Ⓑ The cold, dusty bedroom had pinkish walls, a fireplace, a large bed, several chairs, and a wardrobe.
- Ⓒ The room was dusty and abandoned.
- Ⓓ The room was quiet, lonely and cold and was dominated by a large bed and several red chairs.

5. **Where can you infer this story takes place?**   (RL.7.3)

- Ⓐ In a hotel in the present
- Ⓑ In a home in the future
- Ⓒ In a large home in the past
- Ⓓ In a country cottage in the present

6. **Which line or lines from the excerpt best support the time in which this story is set?**   (RL.7.3)

- Ⓐ This room was chilled, because it seldom had a fire; it was silent, because removed from the nursery and kitchen; solemn, because it was known to be so seldom entered.
- Ⓑ The red-room was a square chamber, very seldom slept in, I might say never, indeed, unless when a chance influx of visitors at Gateshead Hall rendered it necessary to turn to account all the accommodation it contained
- Ⓒ A bed supported on massive pillars of mahogany, hung with curtains of deep red damask, stood out like a tabernacle in the centre; the two large windows, with their blinds always drawn down, were half shrouded in festoons and falls of similar drapery;
- Ⓓ Scarcely less prominent was an ample cushioned easy-chair near the head of the bed, also white, with a footstool before it; and looking, as I thought, like a pale throne.

NOTES

"The Lament"
by Srvani

100 %

It is twilight. A thick wet snow is slowly twirling around the newly lighted street lamps and lying in soft thin layers on roofs, on horses' backs, on people's shoulders and hats. The cabdriver, Iona Potapov, is quite white and looks like a phantom: he is bent double as far as a human body can bend double; he is seated on his box; he never makes a move. If a whole snowdrift fell on him, it seems as if he would not find it necessary to shake it off. His little horse is also quite white, and remains motionless; its immobility, its angularity and its straight wooden-looking legs, even close by, give it the appearance of a gingerbread horse worth a kopek. It is, no doubt, plunged in deep thought. If you were snatched from the plough, from your usual gray surroundings, and were thrown into this slough full of monstrous lights, unceasing noise and hurrying people, you too would find it difficult not to think.

Iona and his little horse have not moved from their place for a long while. They left their yard before dinner and, up to now, not a fare. The evening mist is descending over the town, the white lights of the lamps are replacing brighter rays, and the hubbub of the street is getting louder.

'Cabby for Viborg Way!' suddenly hears Iona. 'Cabby!'
Iona jumps and, through his snow-covered eyelashes, sees an officer in a greatcoat, with his hood over his head.

'Viborg way!' the officer repeats. 'Are you asleep, eh? Viborg way!'
With a nod of assent Iona picks up the reins, in consequence of which layers of snow slip off the horse's back and neck. The officer seats himself in the sleigh, the cabdriver smacks his lips to encourage his horse, stretches out his neck like a swan, sits up and, more from habit than necessity, brandishes his whip. The little horse also stretches its neck, bends its wooden-looking legs, and makes a move undecidedly.

'What are you doing, werewolf!' is the exclamation Iona hears from the dark mass moving to and fro, as soon as they have started.

'Where the devil are you going? To the r-r-right!'

'You do not know how to drive. Keep to the right!' calls the officer angrily. A coachman from a private carriage swears at him; a passerby, who has run across the road and rubbed his shoulder against the horse's nose, looks at him furiously as he sweeps the snow from his sleeve. Iona shifts about on his seat as if he was on needles, moves his elbows as if he were trying to keep his equilibrium, and gasps about like someone suffocating, who does not understand why and wherefore he is there.
'What scoundrels they all are!' jokes the officer; 'one would think they had all entered into an agreement to jostle you or fall under your horse.'

20

Iona looks around at the officer and moves his lips. He evidently wants to say something but the only sound that issues is a snuffle.
'What?' asks the officer.

Iona twists his mouth into a smile and, with an effort, says hoarsely: 'My son, Barin, died this week.'
Hm! What did he die of?'

Iona turns with his whole body towards his fare and says: 'And who knows! They say high fever. He was three days in the hospital and then died… God's will be done.'

"Turn round! The devil!' sounds from the darkness. 'Have you popped off, old doggie, eh? Use your eyes!'

'Go on, go on,' says the officer, 'otherwise we shall not get there by tomorrow. Hurry up a bit!'
"If you were snatched from the plough, from your usual gray surroundings, and were thrown into this slough full of monstrous lights, unceasing noise and hurrying people, you too would find it difficult not to think."

1. What can be inferred from the first two paragraphs of the passage?   (RL.7.1)

Ⓐ that the cab driver was very sad
Ⓑ that the cabby was from a village or a very small town
Ⓒ that the cab driver did not want to think
Ⓓ that the cab driver was not thinking

2. What event that occurred before the story begins influences the way the character Iona acts in this story?   (RL.7.3)

Ⓐ The death of his son
Ⓑ The winter storm
Ⓒ The officer's harsh comments
Ⓓ Iona's wife's sickness

3. Based on the plot of this story, what can you assume was The Lament mentioned in the title?   (RL.7.3)

Ⓐ The officer had to reach Viborg urgently.
Ⓑ Grief made the cabby confused.
Ⓒ The people were sad because the cabby was not driving carefully.
Ⓓ The horse was lost.

4. Which detail in the above passage tells us this story is set in the winter?   (RL.7.3)

Ⓐ It is twilight.

Ⓑ His little horse is also quite white, and remains motionless;

● A thick wet snow is slowly twirling around the newly lighted street lamps and lying in soft thin layers on roofs, on horses' backs, on people's shoulders and hats.

Ⓓ The cabdriver, Iona Potapov, is quite white and looks like a phantom: he is bent double as far as a human body can bend double;

5. What details in the above story tell us that this story's setting is Russia?   (RL.7.3)

● The name of the cab driver, Iona Potapov.

Ⓑ A police officer asks for a cab ride.

Ⓒ It is snowing heavily.

Ⓓ The name of the place the officer wants to go.

"Bruno the Bear"
Excerpt from *The Bond of Love*

I WILL begin with Bruno; my wife's pet sloth bear. I got him for her by an accident. Two years ago we were passing through the cornfields near a small town in Iowa. People were driving away the wild pigs from the fields by shooting at them. Some were shot and some escaped. We thought that everything was over when suddenly a black sloth bear came out panting in the hot sun.

Now I will not shoot a sloth bear wantonly but unfortunately for the poor beast, one of my companions did not feel the same way about it, and promptly shot the bear on the spot.

As we watched the fallen animal we were surprised to see that the black fur on its back moved and left the prostrate body. Then we saw it was a baby bear that had been riding on its mother's back when the sudden shot had killed her. The little creature ran around its prostrate parent making a pitiful noise. I ran up to it to attempt a capture. It scooted into the sugarcane field. Following it with my companions, I was at last able to grab it by the scruff of its neck while it snapped and tried to scratch me with its long, hooked claws. We put it in one of the large jute-bags we had brought and when I got back home I duly presented it to my wife. She was delighted! She at once put a blue colored ribbon around its neck, and after discovering the cub was a 'boy' she christened it Bruno.

Bruno soon took to drinking milk from a bottle. It was but a step further and within a very few days he started eating and drinking everything else. And everything is the right word, for he ate porridge made from any ingredients, vegetables, fruit, nuts, meat (especially pork), curry and rice regardless of condiments and chilies, bread, eggs, chocolates, sweets, pudding, ice-cream, etc., etc., etc. As for drink: milk, tea, coffee, lime juice, aerated water, buttermilk, beer, alcoholic liquor and, in fact, anything liquid. It all went down with relish.

The bear became very attached to our two dogs and to all the children living in and around our farm. He was left quite free in his younger days and spent his time in playing, running into the kitchen and going to sleep in our beds.

One day an accident befell him. I put down poison (barium carbonate) to kill the rats and mice that had got into my library. Bruno entered the library as he often did, and ate some of the poison. Paralysis set in to the extent that he could not stand on his feet. But he dragged himself on his stumps to my wife, who called me. I guessed what had happened.

Off I rushed him in the car to the vet's residence. A case of poisoning! Tame Bear—barium carbonate—what to do? Out came his medical books, and a feverish reference to index began: "What poison did you say, sir?" he asked

"Barium carbonate" I said.

"Ah yes—B—Ba—Barium Salts—Ah! Barium carbonate! Symptoms— paralysis—treatment— injections of ... Just a minute, sir. I'll bring my syringe and the medicine." Said the doc. I dashed back to the car. Bruno was still floundering about on his stumps, but clearly he was weakening rapidly; there was some vomiting, he was breathing heavily, with heaving flanks and gaping mouth. I was really scared and did not know what to do. I was feeling very guilty and was running in and out of the vet's house doing everything the doc asked me.

"Hold him, everybody!" In goes the hypodermic—Bruno squeals — 10 c.c. of the antidote enters his system without a drop being wasted. Ten minutes later: condition unchanged! Another 10 c.c. Injected! Ten minutes later: breathing less torturous— Bruno can move his arms and legs a little although he cannot stand yet. Thirty minutes later: Bruno gets up and has a great feed! He looks at us disdainfully, as much as to say, 'What's barium carbonate to a big black bear like me?' Bruno was still eating. I was really happy to see him recover.

The months rolled on and Bruno had grown many times the size he was when he came. He had equaled the big dogs in height and had even outgrown them. But was just as sweet, just as mischievous, just as playful. And he was very fond of us all. Above all, he loved my wife, and she loved him too! And he could do a few tricks, too. At the command, 'Bruno, wrestle', or 'Bruno, box,' he vigorously tackled anyone who came forward for a rough and tumble. Give him a stick and say 'Bruno, hold gun', and he pointed the stick at you. Ask him, 'Bruno, where's baby?' and he immediately produced and cradled affectionately a stump of wood which he had carefully concealed in his straw bed. But because of the neighborhoods' and our renters' children, poor Bruno, had to be kept chained most of the time.

Then my son and I advised my wife, and friends advised her too, to give Bruno to the zoo. He was getting too big to keep at home. After some weeks of such advice she at last consented. Hastily, and before she could change her mind, a letter was written to the curator of the zoo. Did he want a tame bear for his collection? He replied, "Yes". The zoo sent a cage in a truck, a distance of hundred – eighty – seven miles, and Bruno was packed off.

We all missed him greatly; but in a sense we were relieved. My wife was inconsolable. She wept and fretted. For the first few days she would not eat a thing. Then she wrote a number of letters to the curator. How was Bruno? Back came the replies,

"Well, but fretting; he refuses food too."

After that, friends visiting the zoo were begged to make a point of seeing how Bruno was getting along. They reported that he was well but looked very thin and sad. All the keepers at the zoo said he was fretting. For three months I managed to restrain my wife from visiting the zoo. Then she said one day, "I must see Bruno. Either you take me by car; or I will go myself by bus or train myself." So

I took her by car. Friends had conjectured that the bear would not recognize her. I had thought so too. But while she was yet some yards from his cage Bruno saw her and recognized her. He howled with happiness. She ran up to him, petted him through the bars, and he stood on his head in delight.

For the next three hours she would not leave that cage. She gave him tea, lemonade, cakes, ice cream and what not. Then 'closing time' came and we had to leave. My wife cried bitterly; Bruno cried bitterly; even the hardened curator and the keepers felt depressed. As for me, I had reconciled myself to what I knew was going to happen next.

"Oh please, sir," she asked the curator, "may I have my Bruno back"?
Hesitantly, he answered, "Madam, he belongs to the zoo and is Government property now. I cannot give away Government property. But if my boss, the superintendent agrees, certainly you may have him back."

There followed the return journey home and a visit to the superintendent's office. A tearful pleading: "Bruno and I are both fretting for each other. Will you please give him back to me?" He was a kind-hearted man and consented. Not only that, but he wrote to the curator telling him to lend us a cage for transporting the bear back home.

Back we went to the zoo again, armed with the superintendent's letter. Bruno was driven into a small cage and hoisted on top of the car; the cage was tied securely, and a slow and careful return journey back home was accomplished.

Once home, a squad of workers were engaged for special work around our yard. An island was made for Bruno. It was twenty feet long and fifteen feet wide, and was surrounded by a dry moat, six feet wide and seven feet deep. A wooden box that once housed fowls was brought and put on the island for Bruno to sleep in at night. Straw was placed inside to keep him warm, and his 'baby', the gnarled stump, along with his 'gun', the piece of bamboo, both of which had been sentimentally preserved since he had been sent away to the zoo, were put back for him to play with. In a few days the workers hoisted the cage on to the island and Bruno was released. He was delighted; standing on his hind legs, he pointed his 'gun' and cradled his 'baby'. My wife spent hours sitting on a chair there while he sat on her lap. He was fifteen months old and pretty heavy too!

The way my wife reaches the island and leaves it is interesting. I have tied a rope to the overhanging branch of a maple tree with a loop at its end. Putting one foot in the loop, she kicks off with the other, to bridge the six-foot gap that constitutes the width of the surrounding moat. The return journey back is made the same way.

But who can say now that a sloth bear has no sense of affection, no memory and no individual characteristics?

1. How can the reader infer the bear was depressed?   (RL.7.1)

Ⓐ because both the bear and the author's wife cried bitterly while departing
Ⓑ because the bear did not recognize its mistress
Ⓒ because the author's wife was lean and depressed
● because Bruno would not eat anything.

2. Which of the following would make the best alternate title for this selection?   (RL.7.2)

Ⓐ The Pet
● Hungry for Love
Ⓒ The Author's Wife
Ⓓ The Animal in the Zoo

3. What is this story mostly about?   (RL.7.2)

Ⓐ about having a bear as a pet and how to care for it
● about the bond that the bear and the author's wife shared
Ⓒ about rescuing a bear
Ⓓ about animals

4. What event in the plot of this story led Bruno to be taken to the Vet's house?   (RL.7.3)

Ⓐ He ate too much food.
● He ate a rat poison called barium carbonate and was paralyzed.
Ⓒ He broke his leg trying wrestle.
Ⓓ None of these.

5. What motivated the narrator to keep Bruno chained up?   (RL.7.3)

Ⓐ because he had grown big
● because he was very playful and this scared some of the children in the neighbor hood
Ⓒ because he was very dangerous
Ⓓ because he was a bear

6. What is the central idea of bold typed portion of the passage?   (RI.7.2)

Ⓐ Bruno eats rat poison, but doesn't die.
Ⓑ An accident almost causes the narrator's family to lose its pet.
Ⓒ A vet treats a pet bear.
Ⓓ The narrator feels guilty about accidentally poisoning his pet bear.

7. Which quality does barium carbonate NOT have?   (RI.7.4)

Ⓐ It is poisonous to animals.
Ⓑ It is used to get rid of rodents.
Ⓒ It is safe for animals except rodents.
Ⓓ It can cause paralysis.

Best Friends to Boyfriend/Girlfriend

Ever since they were kids, Julie and Max had been best friends. They went to kindergarten together. They went to summer camp together, They hung out together every weekend. But suddenly, things between the two had started to change.

Max had started playing on the football team and didn't have much time for Julie anymore. He was always busy, and he never seemed to make it to study hall, where the two used to swap stories about their favorite (or least favorite) teachers. In class, Julie noticed that Max never seemed to have his homework done on time anymore. She even noticed that he got a D on his last paper. She knew something was going on with him – but what?

At first, Julie decided to play it cool and see how things went. She tried waiting in the hall for Max after class to see if she could ask if he was OK. But days went by, and he never had time to stop. He'd rush right past her in the hall, only to leave her feeling even worse about what was happening between them.

Even though she wasn't sure she could handle the situation herself, Julie didn't want to talk to her parents because she was afraid they would tell her not to hang out with Max anymore. She barely saw him as it was, so she knew it would just make things worse if her parents didn't approve of him. She didn't want to tell Max's parents either because she didn't want him to get in trouble. Still, it seemed like something needed to change. Julie decided to go to one of her school counselors and let her know she was concerned.

When she walked into Mrs. Smith's room, she was surprised to see that Max was already sitting there.

"I'm sorry, I'll come back," Julie said.

"No, stay," said Max. "Maybe you can help."

Julie was surprised to find that Max had visited the counselor's office for the same reason she had: He was starting to feel overwhelmed with all of the things he was supposed to be doing as a student, an athlete and a friend. He needed some guidance on how to determine what truly mattered, and how to divide his time between all of the things that were important to him. When she realized that Max was still the same old Max (just a little more stressed), Julie was relieved. She was also happy to know that he had come to the conclusion on his own, without her having to talk to someone else about it. She decided it was a sign they were both growing up.

http://www.fanfiction.net/s/5080637/6/Best-Friends-to-BoyfriendGirlfriend

1. What can you infer about relationship between Julie and Max?   (RL.7.1)

Ⓐ They were best of friends who cared about each other.
Ⓑ They really hated each other, so they went to the counselor alone.
Ⓒ They were just acquaintances who only occasionally talked.
Ⓓ They were neighbors.

2. How does Max playing football affect his relationship with Julie in this story?   (RL.7.3)

Ⓐ It brings the two of them closer together.
Ⓑ It gives the two something to talk about during study hall.
Ⓒ It makes Julie jealous.
Ⓓ It keeps the two of them from spending time together.

3. How would the outcome of the selection be different if the final scene was set in the principal's office instead of the guidance counselor's office?   (RL.7.3)

Ⓐ Julie may not have been as sympathetic to Max because he would have been in trouble with the principal.
Ⓑ Max would have been embarrassed because Julie saw him in the principal's office.
Ⓒ The outcome of the selection wouldn't change if the setting changed.
Ⓓ The outcome would change with any setting/ending different than the counselor's office.

4. What events in the story did NOT contribute to the character of Max being overwhelmed?   (RL.7.3)

Ⓐ work commitments
Ⓑ school commitments
Ⓒ sports commitments
Ⓓ parent's expectations

5. Which of the following is NOT an event in the story that leads Julie to become worried about Max?   (RL.7.3)

Ⓐ He was getting bad grades.
Ⓑ He wasn't doing his homework.
Ⓒ He had lost weight.
Ⓓ He was too busy for her.

6. Who are the two main characters of the above story?   (RL.7.3)

- Ⓐ Max and the counselor
- Ⓑ Max
- Ⓒ Max and Julie
- Ⓓ Julie and the counselor

NOTES

THE OLD MAN AND THE DEVILS - A Gaelic Folk Tale
(Ed. Kate Douglas Wiggin)

A long time ago there was an old man who had a big lump on the right side of his face. One day he went into the mountain to cut wood, when the rain began to pour and the wind to blow so very hard that, finding it impossible to return home, and filled with fear, he took refuge in the hollow of an old tree. While sitting there doubled up and unable to sleep, he heard the confused sound of many voices in the distance gradually approaching to where he was. He said to himself: "How strange! I thought I was all alone in the mountain, but I hear the voices of many people." So, taking courage, he peeped out, and saw a great crowd of strange-looking beings. Some were red, and dressed in green clothes; others were black, and dressed in red clothes; some had only one eye; others had no mouth; indeed, it is quite impossible to describe their varied and strange looks. They kindled a fire, so that it became as light as day. They sat down in two cross-rows, and began to drink wine and make merry just like human beings. They passed the wine cup around so often that many of them soon drank too much. One of the young devils got up and began to sing a merry song and to dance; so also many others; some danced well, others badly. One said: "We have had uncommon fun to-night, but I would like to see something new."

Then the old man, losing all fear, thought he would like to dance, and saying, "Let come what will, if I die for it, I will have a dance, too," crept out of the hollow tree and, with his cap slipped over his nose and his ax sticking in his belt, began to dance. The devils in great surprise jumped up, saying, "Who is this?" but the old man advancing and receding, swaying to and fro, and posturing this way and that way, the whole crowd laughed and enjoyed the fun, saying: "How well the old man dances! You must always come and join us in our sport; but, for fear you might not come, you must give us a pledge that you will. " So the devils consulted together, and, agreeing that the lump on his face, which was a token of wealth, was what he valued most highly, demanded that it should be taken. The old man replied: "I have had this lump many years, and would not without good reason part with it; but you may have it, or an eye, or my nose either if you wish." So the devils laid hold of it, twisting and pulling, and took it off without giving him any pain, and put it away as a pledge that he would come back. Just then the day began to dawn, and the birds to sing, so the devils hurried away.

The old man felt his face and found it quite smooth, and not a trace of the lump left. He forgot all about cutting wood, and hastened home. His wife, seeing him, exclaimed in great surprise, "What has happened to you?" So he told her all that had befallen him.

Now, among the neighbors there was another old man who had a big lump on the left side of his face. Hearing all about how the first old man had got rid of his misfortune, he determined that he would also try the same plan. So he went and crept into the hollow tree, and waited for the devils to come. Sure enough, they came just as he was told, and they sat down, drank wine, and made merry just as they did before. The second old man, afraid and trembling, crept out of the hollow tree. The devils welcomed him, saying: "The old man has come; now let us see him dance." This old fellow was awkward, and did not dance as well as the other, so the devils cried out: "You dance badly, and are getting worse and worse; we will give you back the lump which we took from you as a pledge." Upon this, one of the devils brought the lump, and stuck it on the other side of his face; so the poor old fellow returned home with a lump on each side.

1. Which is the best summary of the second paragraph of the story?   (RL.7.2)

Ⓐ Two men who have deformities are "cured" in different ways by a group of devils.
Ⓑ An old man with a lump on his face dances freely with a group of devils.
Ⓒ An old man dances freely and is rewarded for his talent by a group of devils who cure him of a deformity that never really bothered him.
Ⓓ The old man returns to his home free of the lump on his face. His wife is shocked by his transformation.

2. What is the theme of this selection?   (RL.7.2)

Ⓐ Dance as if no one is watching.
Ⓑ To be healed, you have to make a deal with the Devil.
Ⓒ Blessings come to people who don't expect them.
Ⓓ Changing your appearance will only bring you misery.

3. Based on information in the selection, what event can you assume happened between the first man returning without the lump on his face and the second man heading to the tree in hopes of having his lump removed?   (RL.7.3)

Ⓐ The people in town began gossiping about how the first man lost his lump.
Ⓑ The old man's wife celebrated her husband losing his lump.
Ⓒ The second old man prayed he would lose his lump.
Ⓓ The devils decided to punish the next man who tried to dance with them.

MY SHADOW by Robert Louis Stevenson

I have a little shadow that goes in and out with me,
And what can be the use of him is more than I can see.

He is very, very like me, from the heels up to the head;
And I see him jump before me, when I jump into my bed.

The funniest thing about him is the way he likes to grow—
Not at all like proper children, which is always very slow;

For he sometimes shoots up taller, like an India-rubber ball,
And he sometimes gets so little that there's none of him at all.

5. Which sentence best summarizes this selection?   (RL.7.2)

Ⓐ A little boy who does not understand shadows delights in playing with his shadow.
Ⓑ A little boy plays with a friend.
Ⓒ A little boy is confused by the shadow that is following him around as he plays.
Ⓓ A little boy tries to control his shadow as he plays.

8. The narrator of this poem is a child. How does this character affect the plot of the poem?
                                                                        (RL.7.3)

Ⓐ He is confused by his shadow, so he is constantly trying to avoid it.
Ⓑ He is amazed by his shadow, so plays with it to try to understand it.
Ⓒ He is frightened by his shadow, so he tries to "lose" it.

THE WONDERFUL HAIR by A. H. Wraitslaw

There was a man who was very poor, but so well supplied with children that he was utterly unable to maintain them, and one morning more than once prepared to kill them, in order not to see their misery in dying of hunger, but his wife prevented him. One night a child came to him in his sleep, and said to him: "Man! I see that you are making up your mind to destroy and to kill your poor little children, and I know that you are distressed there at; but in the morning you will find under your pillow a mirror, a red kerchief, and an embroidered pocket-handkerchief; take all three secretly and tell nobody; then go to such a hill; by it you will find a stream; go along it till you come to its fountain-head; there you will find a damsel as bright as the sun, with her hair hanging down over her back. Be on your guard, that the ferocious she-dragon do not coil round you; do not converse with her if she speaks; for if you converse with her, she will poison you, and turn you into a fish or something else, and will then devour you but if she bids you examine her head, examine it, and as you turn over her hair, look, and you will find one hair as red as blood; pull it out and run back again; then, if she suspects and begins to run after you, throw her first the embroidered pocket-handkerchief, then the kerchief, and, lastly, the mirror; then she will find occupation for herself. And sell that hair to some rich man; but don't let them cheat you, for that hair is worth countless wealth; and you will thus enrich yourself and maintain your children."

When the poor man awoke, he found everything under his pillow, just as the child had told him in his sleep; and then he went to the hill. When there, he found the stream, went on and on alongside of it, till he came to the fountain-head. Having looked about him to see where the damsel was, he espied her above a piece of water, like sunbeams threaded on a needle, and she was embroidering at a frame on stuff, the threads of which were young men's hair. As soon as he saw her, he made a reverence to her, and she stood on her feet and questioned him: "Whence are you, unknown young man?" But he held his tongue. She questioned him again: "Who are you? Why have you come?" and much else of all sorts; but he was as mute as a stone, making signs with his hands, as if he were deaf and wanted help. Then she told him to sit down on her skirt. He did not wait for any more orders, but sat down, and she bent down her head to him, that he might examine it. Turning over the hair of her head, as if to examine it, he was not long in finding that red hair, and separated it from the other hair, pulled it out, jumped off her skirt and ran away back as he best could. She noticed it, and ran at his heels full speed after him. He looked round, and seeing that she was about to overtake him, threw, as he was told, the embroidered pocket-handkerchief on the way, and when she saw the pocket-handkerchief she stooped and began to overhaul it in every direction, admiring the embroidery, till he had got a good way off. Then the damsel placed the pocket-handkerchief in her bosom, and ran after him again.

When he saw that she was about to overtake him, he threw the red kerchief, and she again occupied herself, admiring and gazing, till the poor man had again got a good way off. Then the damsel became exasperated, and threw both the pocket-handkerchief and the kerchief on the way, and ran after him in pursuit. Again, when he saw that she was about to overtake him, he threw the mirror. When the damsel came to the mirror, the like of which she had never seen before, she lifted it up, and when she saw herself in it, not knowing that it was herself, but thinking that it was somebody else, she, as it were, fell in love with herself in the mirror, and the man got so far off that she was no longer able to overtake him. When she saw that she could not catch him, she turned back, and the man reached his home safe and sound. After arriving at his home, he showed his wife the hair, and told her all that had happened to him, but she began to jeer and laugh at him. But he paid no attention to her, and went to a town to sell the hair. A crowd of all sorts of people and merchants collected round him; one offered a sequin, another two, and so on, higher and higher, till they came to a hundred gold sequins. Just then the emperor heard of the hair, summoned the man into his presence, and said to him that he would give him a thousand sequins for it, and he sold it to him. What was the hair? The emperor split it in two from top to bottom, and found registered in it in writing many remarkable things, which happened in the olden time since the beginning of the world. Thus the man became rich and lived on with his wife and children. And that child, that came to him in his sleep, was an angel sent by the Lord God, whose will it was to aid the poor man, and to reveal secrets which had not been revealed till then.

1. Which best summarizes the directions the child gives the poor man while he is sleeping?
(RL.7.2)

Ⓐ   Go to the stream and find a damsel who will give you a great deal of money.
Ⓑ   You should not kill your children because there is a damsel at the stream who will help you by giving you a lock of her hair.
Ⓒ   You will find a hair masked as blood that will cause you great trouble.
Ⓓ   At the stream, there is a damsel who can help you make money for your family. You must not speak to her and may need to trick her to get a piece of her hair that you can sell for a great deal of money.

2. What is one theme of this story?
(RL.7.2)

Ⓐ   It is wrong for a parent to want to hurt his children.
Ⓑ   The things we do for family can bring about great wealth for many.
Ⓒ   God rewards those who protect their children.
Ⓓ   His character does not have any influence on the plot.

3. How does the little child affect the plot of the story?
(RL.7.3)

Ⓐ   He makes his father feel guilty for wanting to kill his children.
Ⓑ   He foreshadows the future events in the story.
Ⓒ   He falsely predicts what will happen to his father later in the story.
Ⓓ   His character does not have any influence on the plot.

4. What detail from this story does NOT help the reader see that it takes place in a rural (country) setting?   (RL.7.3)

   Ⓐ The characters live near a stream.
   Ⓑ He is going to sell hair in a local market.
   Ⓒ He has many children.
   Ⓓ He is to go into the woods/forest.

5. What is the tone at the end of this story?   (RL.7.4)

   Ⓐ Serious
   Ⓑ Joyful
   Ⓒ Angry
   Ⓓ Confused

6. How is the outcome of this selection different than what the little boy predicted when he spoke to his father through a dream?   (RL.7.7)

   Ⓐ The father is not able to earn a great deal of money by selling the damsel's hair.
   Ⓑ The damsel comes after the father and attacks him.
   Ⓒ The boy's prediction is accurate. There is no difference.
   Ⓓ The father is not happy with the boy's instructions.

"The Smith and the Fairies": A Gaelic Folk Tale
(Ed. Kate Douglas Wiggin)

Years ago there lived in Crossbrig a smith of the name of MacEachern. This man had an only child, a boy of about thirteen or fourteen years of age, cheerful, strong, and healthy. All of a sudden he fell ill; took to his bed and moped whole days away. No one could tell what was the matter with him, and the boy himself could not, or would not, tell how he felt. He was wasting away fast; getting thin, old, and yellow; and his father and all his friends were afraid that he would die.

At last one day, after the boy had been lying in this condition for a long time, getting neither better nor worse, always confined to bed, but with an extraordinary appetite—one day, while sadly revolving these things, and standing idly at his forge, with no heart to work, the smith was agreeably surprised to see an old man, well known for his sagacity and knowledge of out-of-the-way things, walk into his workshop. Forthwith he told him the occurrence which had clouded his life.

The old man looked grave as he listened; and after sitting a long time pondering over all he had heard, gave his opinion thus: "It is not your son you have got. The boy has been carried away by the 'Daione Sith,' and they have left a Sibhreach in his place."

"Alas! and what then am I to do?" said the smith. "How am I ever to see my own son again?"

"I will tell you how," answered the old man. "But, first, to make sure that it is not your own son you have got, take as many empty egg-shells as you can get, go into his room, spread them out carefully before his sight, then proceed to draw water with them, carrying them two and two in your hands as if they were a great weight, and arrange them when full, with every sort of earnestness around the fire." The smith accordingly gathered as many broken egg-shells as he could get, went into the room, and proceeded to carry out all his instructions.

He had not been long at work before there arose from the bed a shout of laughter, and the voice of the seeming sick boy exclaimed, "I am eight hundred years of age, and I have never seen the like of that before." The smith returned and told the old man.

"Well, now," said the sage to him, "did I not tell you that it was not your son you had: your son is in Borracheill in a digh there (that is, a round green hill frequented by fairies). Get rid as soon as possible of this intruder, and I think I may promise you your son. You must light a very large and bright fire before the bed on which this stranger is lying. He will ask you, 'What is the use of such a fire as that?' Answer him at once, 'You will see that presently!' and then seize him, and throw him into the middle of it. If it is your own son you have got, he will call out to you to save him; but if not, the thing will fly through the roof."

The smith again followed the old man's advice: kindled a large fire, answered the question put to him as he had been directed to do, and seizing the child flung him in without hesitation. The Sibhreach gave an awful yell, and sprang through the roof, where a hole had been left to let the smoke out.

On a certain night the old man told him the green round hill, where the fairies kept the boy, would be open, and on that date the smith, having provided himself with a Bible, a dirk, and a crowing cock, was to proceed to the hill. He would hear singing and dancing, and much merriment going on, he had been told, but he was to advance boldly; the Bible he carried would be a certain safeguard to him against any danger from the fairies. On entering the hill he was to stick the dirk in the threshold, to prevent the hill from closing upon him; "and then," continued the old man, "on entering you will see a spacious apartment before you, beautifully clean, and there, standing far within, working at a forge, you will also see your own son. When you are questioned, say you come to seek him, and will not go without him."

Not long after this, the time came round, and the smith sallied forth, prepared as instructed. Sure enough as he approached the hill, there was a light where light was seldom seen before. Soon after, a sound of piping, dancing, and joyous merriment reached the anxious father on the night wind.

Overcoming every impulse to fear, the smith approached the threshold steadily, stuck the dirk into it as directed, and entered. Protected by the Bible he carried on his breast, the fairies could not touch him; but they asked him, with a good deal of displeasure, what he wanted there. He answered, "I want my son, whom I see down there, and I will not go without him."

Upon hearing this the whole company before him gave a loud laugh, which wakened up the cock he carried dozing in his arms, who at once leaped up on his shoulders, clapped his wings lustily, and crowed loud and long.

The fairies, incensed, seized the smith and his son, and throwing them out of the hill, flung the dirk after them, and in an instant all was dark.

For a year and a day the boy never did a turn of work, and hardly ever spoke a word; but at last one day, sitting by his father and watching him finishing a sword he was making for some chief, and which he was very particular about, he suddenly exclaimed, "That is not the way to do it;" and taking the tools from his father's hands he set to work himself in his place, and soon fashioned a sword, the like of which was never seen in the country before.

From that day the young man wrought constantly with his father, and became the inventor of a peculiarly fine and well-tempered weapon, the making of which kept the two smiths, father and son, in constant employment, spread their fame far and wide, and gave them the means in abundance, as they before had the disposition, to live content with all the world and very happily with each other.

1. Which sentence best summarizes from the second to last paragraph in this story? (RL.7.2)

Ⓐ The smith's son returns to his father and does not speak for a year and a day.
Ⓑ The smith's son criticizes his father's work.
Ⓒ When the smith's son finally speaks after a year and one day of silence, he offers valuable advice to his father on how to make a sword.
Ⓓ The smith's son has nothing to say until he sees his father not doing his best work.

2. Which detail from the story is NOT a clue that the story is set in the past? (RL.7.3)

Ⓐ There are no longer smiths working today.
Ⓑ People in the story believe there are fairies in the woods.
Ⓒ The smith carries a Bible with him because he believes it will protect him.
Ⓓ The smith and his son make swords for people in town.

3. How is the fairy pretend version of the smith's son different than the smith's actual son?
(RL.7.7)

Ⓐ The fairy is a humorous trickster, while the real son is quiet and serious.
Ⓑ The fairy is cruel to the father, while the real son is kind to his father.
Ⓒ The fairy and the son are exactly alike.
Ⓓ The fairy and the father are alike.

HOW WISDOM BECAME THE PROPERTY OF THE HUMAN RACE
(West African Folktale)

THERE once lived, in Fanti-land, a man named Father Anansi. He possessed all the wisdom in the world. People came to him daily for advice and help.

One day the men of the country were unfortunate enough to offend Father Anansi, who immediately resolved to punish them. After much thought he decided that the severest penalty he could inflict would be to hide all his wisdom from them. He set to work at once to gather again all that he had already given. When he had succeeded, as he thought, in collecting it, he placed all in one great pot. This he carefully sealed, and determined to put it in a spot where no human being could reach it.

Now, Father Anansi had a son, whose name was Kweku Tsin. This boy began to suspect his father of some secret design, so he made up his mind to watch carefully.

Next day he saw his father quietly slip out of the house, with his precious pot hung round his neck. Kweku Tsin followed. Father Anansi went through the forest till he had left the village far behind.

Then, selecting the highest and most inaccessible-looking tree, he began to climb. The heavy pot, hanging in front of him, made his ascent almost impossible. Again and again he tried to reach the top of the tree, where he intended to hang the pot. There, he thought, Wisdom would indeed be beyond the reach of everyone but himself. He was unable, however, to carry out his desire. At each trial the pot swung in his way.

For some time Kweku Tsin watched his father's vain attempts. At last, unable to contain himself any longer, he cried out: "Father, why do you not hang the pot on your back? Then you could easily climb the tree."

Father Anansi turned and said: "I thought I had all the world's wisdom in this pot. But I find you possess more than I do. All my wisdom was insufficient to show me what to do, yet you have been able to tell me." In his anger he threw the pot down. It struck on a great rock and broke. The wisdom contained in it escaped and spread throughout the world.

1. Which sentence best summarizes the first paragraph? (RL.7.2)

Ⓐ Father Anansi wanted to teach the men a lesson.
Ⓑ The men wanted Father Anansi to provide them with wisdom and he refused.
Ⓒ To punish the men for offending him, Father Anansi hid all of his wisdom where they could not find it.
Ⓓ Father Anansi hid away all of his wisdom until the men apologized.

2. Which sentence best summarizes what Kweku Tsin saw when he followed his father?

(RL.7.2)

Ⓐ Kweku Tsin saw his father climb the tallest tree in the forest.
Ⓑ Kweku Tsin watched as father tried and failed to reach the top of the tallest tree.
Ⓒ Kewku Tsin watched his father hide the pot of wisdom
Ⓓ Kweku Tisin taught his father his lesson.

3. What is the climax of this story?

(RL.7.3)

Ⓐ When Kweku Tsin follows his father into the forest
Ⓑ When Kweku Tsin gives his father advice on how to carry the pot to the top of the tree
Ⓒ When Father Anansi threw the pot to the ground
Ⓓ When Father Anansi decided to hide the wisdom from the men

NOTES

"The Land of Nod"
by Robert Louis Stevenson

From breakfast on through all the day
At home among my friends I stay,
But every night I go abroad
Afar into the Land of Nod.

All by myself I have to go,
With none to tell me what to do—
All alone beside the streams
And up the mountain-sides of dreams.

The strangest things are there for me,
Both things to eat and things to see,
And many frightening sights abroad
Till morning in the Land of Nod.

Try as I like to find the way,
I never can get back by day,
Nor can remember plain and clear
The curious music that I hear.

1. What is the theme of this selection?   (RL.7.2)

  Ⓐ When we nod our heads, we get to see new places.
  Ⓑ Dreams let you travel to new and magical places.
  Ⓒ Traveling to the Land of Nod is exciting.
  Ⓓ People can travel anywhere they want to go.

2. What is the setting of this poem?   (RL.7.3)

  Ⓐ A child's bedroom
  Ⓑ A child's dreams
  Ⓒ The mountains
  Ⓓ The breakfast table

44

The Two Melons A Chinese Folk Tale
(Ed. Kate Douglas Wiggin)

An honest and poor old woman was washing clothes at a pool, when a bird that a hunter had disabled by a shot in the wing, fell down into the water before her. She gently took up the bird, carried it home with her, dressed its wound, and fed it until it was well, when it soared away. Some days later it returned, put before her an oval seed, and departed again. The woman planted the seed in her yard and when it came up she recognized the leaf as that of a melon. She made a trellis for it, and gradually a fruit formed on it, and grew to great size.

Toward the end of the year, the old dame was unable to pay her debts, and her poverty so weighed upon her that she became ill. Sitting one day at her door, feverish and tired, she saw that the melon was ripe, and looked luscious; so she determined to try its unknown quality. Taking a knife, she severed the melon from its stalk, and was surprised to hear it chink in her hands. On cutting it in two, she found it full of silver and gold pieces, with which she paid her debts and bought supplies for many days.

Among her neighbours was a busybody who craftily found out how the old woman had so suddenly become rich. Thinking there was no good reason why she should not herself be equally fortunate, she washed clothes at the pool, keeping a sharp lookout for birds until she managed to hit and maim one of a flock that was flitting over the water. She then took the disabled bird home, and treated it with care till its wing healed and it flew away. Shortly afterward it came back with a seed in its beak, laid it before her, and again took flight. The woman quickly planted the seed, saw it come up and spread its leaves, made a trellis for it, and had the gratification of seeing a melon form on its stalk. In prospect of her future wealth, she ate rich food, bought fine garments, and got so deeply into debt that, before the end of the year, she was harried by duns. But the melon grew apace, and she was delighted to find that, as it ripened, it became of vast size, and that when she shook it there was a great rattling inside. At the end of the year she cut it down, and divided it, expecting it to be a coffer of coins; but there crawled out of it two old, lame, hungry beggars, who told her they would remain and eat at her table as long as they lived.

1. Where and when can you infer this story takes place?   (RL.7.3)

Ⓐ In the past in a bustling city
Ⓑ In the past in a poor village
Ⓒ In the recent past in a rural area
Ⓓ In the present in a farming community

2. How are the busybody neighbour and the honest old woman different? (RL.7.7)

Ⓐ They are not different. They are both poor and hungry.
Ⓑ The honest old woman acts out of selflessness while the busybody neighbour acts out of self-interest.
Ⓒ The honest old woman is much poorer than the busybody neighbour.
Ⓓ The honest old woman minds her own business while the busybody neighbour is concerned with everyone else's business.

3. How would this story be different if the busybody neighbour was the first to receive a melon seed? (RL.7.7)

Ⓐ She would have gotten a garden full of melons to eat and the old, honest woman would be left with a garden full of beggars.
Ⓑ Both the busybody neighbour and the old, honest woman would no longer be poor.
Ⓒ There would be no difference. The busybody neighbour would have still gotten a garden of beggars because of the way she went about getting her melon seed.
Ⓓ The busybody would tell everyone about the melon.

"Base Details"
by Siegfried Sassoon

IF I were fierce, and bald, and short of breath,
I'd live with scarlet Majors at the Base,
And speed glum heroes up the line to death.

You'd see me with my puffy petulant face,
Guzzling and gulping in the best hotel,
Reading the Roll of Honour. 'Poor young chap,'
I'd say—'I used to know his father well;
Yes, we've lost heavily in this last scrap.'

And when the war is done and youth stone dead,
I'd toddle safely home and die—in bed.

1. **What is the narrator's tone toward the officers at the base?**   (RL.7.4)

   Ⓐ He respects the decisions they make about the war.
   Ⓑ He looks forward to moving up the ranks and becoming an officer.
   Ⓒ He is an officer and feels his decisions are well-thought out.
   Ⓓ He believes the officers are fat and greedy and don't value the young soldiers.

2. **From which line from the poem can you infer the narrator is disgusted with the officers?**
                                                                              (RL.7.4)

   Ⓐ I'd toddle safely home and die - in bed.

   Ⓑ If I were fierce, and bald, and short of breath,
      I'd live with scarlet Majors at the base...

   Ⓒ You'd see me with my puffy petulant face,
      Guzzling and gulping in the best hotel.

   Ⓓ Yes, we've lost heavily in this last scrap.

3. **Which statement is NOT inferred by this poem?**   (RL.7.7)

Ⓐ He is young and may still be fighting in the war.
Ⓑ He is on the opposite side of the war.
Ⓒ People have died in the war.
Ⓓ The speaker doesn't like the man he describes in the poem

From <u>Guiseppi Verdi</u> by Thomas Trapper

Whenever the organ man came into the village of Roncole, in Italy (where Verdi was born, October 10, 1813), Verdi could not be kept indoors. But he followed the wonderful organ and the wonderful man who played it, all day long, as happy as he could be.

When Giuseppe was seven years old his father, though only a poor innkeeper, bought him a spinet, a sort of small piano. So faithfully did the little boy practise that the spinet was soon quite worn out and new jacks, or hammers, had to be made for it. This was done by Stephen Cavaletti, who wrote a message on one of the jacks telling that he made them anew and covered them with leather, and fixed the pedal, doing all for nothing, because the little boy, Giuseppe Verdi, showed such willingness to practise and to learn. Thus the good Stephen thought this was pay enough.

1. Which sentence from the passage best explains how Verdi felt about his first spinet?

(RI.7.1)

Ⓐ "But he followed the wonderful organ and wonderful man who played it all day long, as happy as he could be."
Ⓑ "So faithfully did the little boy practice that the spinet was soon quite worn out and new jacks, or hammers, had to be made for it."
Ⓒ "…because the little boy, Giuseppe Verdi, showed such willingness to practice and to learn."
Ⓓ "Thus the good Stephen thought this was pay enough."

2. What Is the main idea the writer wants the reader to draw from these paragraphs?

(RI.7.2)

Ⓐ Verdi was drawn and committed to music from an early age.
Ⓑ Verdi was hard on his spinet because he played it every day.
Ⓒ Verdi practiced the spinet for too many hours each day.
Ⓓ Verdi lived in Italy when he was a child.

3. Based on the information in these paragraphs, what musical instrument can you infer the spinet is most like?

(RI.7.4)

Ⓐ A piano
Ⓑ A trumpet
Ⓒ A violin
Ⓓ An electric keyboard

4. **Based on these paragraphs, what can you infer the author's view of Verdi is?** (RI.7.16)

Ⓐ He is amazed by Verdi's talent.
Ⓑ He thinks Verdi started playing an instrument at too young of an age.
Ⓒ He is jealous of Verdi's talent.
Ⓓ He is unsure what to make of Verdi's talent.

5. **If turned into a media production, this passage would most likely be...?** (RI.7.7)

Ⓐ A story on the local news
Ⓑ A play at the local theater
Ⓒ A slideshow presentation
Ⓓ A song about Verdi

Skunk Chow

Skunks are <u>omnivores</u>. They can be found eating nuts, berries, roots, leaves, grasses and even some types of fungi (mushroom-like plants). For animals, they enjoy dining on rodents such as mice and rats, insects, earthworms, frogs, lizards, toads and birds. Sometimes when they are unable to find live animals to eat they become **scavengers** eating dead animals left behind. When they live close to people's homes, skunks sometimes will even get into trash cans, eating garbage.

When skunks eat they do not limit themselves to small meals. They like to "pig out" on whatever food they can find. When there is a large amount of food available skunks get very fat very quickly.

http://en.wikipedia.org/wiki/Skunk

1. If you had to answer the question "Can skunks control their appetites?" which sentence would you use to support your answer? (RI.7.1)

Ⓐ "They can be found eating nuts, berries, roots, leaves, grasses, and even some types of fungi (mushroom-like plants)."

Ⓑ "For animals, they enjoy dining on rodents such as mice and rats, insects, earth worms, frogs, lizards, toads, and birds."

Ⓒ "When they live close to people's homes, skunks sometimes will even get into trash cans, eating garbage."

Ⓓ "They like to 'pig out' on whatever food they can find. When there is a large amount of food, skunks get fat very quickly."

2. If the author removed the sentence telling you skunks were omnivores, could you still infer that skunks are omnivores? (RI.7.1)

Ⓐ No, because the author does not tell me what an omnivore is or what it eats.

Ⓑ No, because the author does not provide enough information about the types of food a skunk eats.

Ⓒ Yes, because the author shows that a skunk eats both plants and animals.

Ⓓ Yes, because the author says that skunks are also scavengers.

3. Based on information in the selection, what does the underlined term mean?   (RI.7.4)

Ⓐ An animal that eats only plants
Ⓑ An animal that eats nuts and berries
Ⓒ An animal that eats plants and meat
Ⓓ An animal that is usually awake only at night

4. Based on information in the selection, what does the bold term mean?   (RI.7.4)

Ⓐ An animal that eats other animals.
Ⓑ An animal that overeats.
Ⓒ An animal that eats meat from carcasses left by other animals.
Ⓓ An animal that eats human garbage.

NOTES

Fall Leaves
USDA Forest Service

We almost always think of trees as being green, but there is one time of year when their leaves turn a myriad orange, red, yellow and brown: the beautiful and chilly days of fall. Those living in the Eastern or Northern United States come to anticipate the change in color starting in September or October every single year. But what causes the leaves to change color, and why?

Just like many animals that hibernate for the winter, trees experience a unique change during the winter months. During summer, for instance, plants use the process of photosynthesis to transform carbon dioxide found in the air into organic compounds like sugars using energy from the sun. During the winter, however, there is less light to go around, and their ability to create food from the photosynthesis process is limited.

What does that have to do with a leaf's color? The substance that allows trees to turn carbon dioxide into food (chlorophyll) is also the cause for the leaf's green sheen. As the photosynthesis process wanes in the colder months due to the lack of sun, so does its greenish hue, allowing other elements present in the leaf to show through. Believe it or not, the yellows and oranges that appear in fall have actually been there all year in the form of nutrients like carotene (also found in carrots). The intense green color of the chlorophyll had simply overshadowed them. But what about the reds and browns? And what causes the leaves to fall away after they change color?

The bright reds and purples in each leaf come from a strong antioxidant that many trees create on their own because of their protective qualities. The antioxidant helps protect the trees from the sun, lower their freezing levels, and protect them from frost. As winter comes, so does the need for the antioxidant (similar to the way a dog gets more fur during winter to stay warmer).

As for the leaves falling, that is another story. At the base of each leaf, there is a layer of cells that carry food and water from the leaf to the tree during the summer months to keep it fed. In the fall, that layer actually starts to harden, preventing the passage of nutrients. Because of this, the nutrients and waste that previously passed from the leaf into the tree become trapped in the leaf with no fresh water to clean it. Not only does this cause the leaf to turn brown, eventually it causes the cells within it to harden so much that the leaf tears and blows away. Thus the pile of leaves you enjoyed jumping in as a child.

Because each tree, and each leaf, contains a unique amount of nutrients depending on how well-nourished it was over the spring and summer, the way each leaf breaks down during the winter months is also quite different. The result is the unique and complex facet of colors we see in each neighborhood or forest each fall.

http://www.sciencemadesimple.com/leaves.htm

1. **What is the main theme of the above passage?** (RI.7.2)

Ⓐ Fall weather
Ⓑ What happens to the leaves during fall
Ⓒ The life cycle of a tree during fall
Ⓓ Weather during fall

2. **If this passage was turned into a video documentary, what would it include to help you understand how the leaves change color?** (RI.7.7)

Ⓐ Time-lapse video of the leaves changing color
Ⓑ Paintings by artists depicting fall leaves
Ⓒ Pictures of animals that hibernate during the winter
Ⓓ Subtitles of the text on the screen

3. **You've been asked to turn this passage into a slide show presentation. Which graphic would you use to help explain the process of leaves changing color?** (RI.7.7)

Ⓐ A picture of leaves that have changed color
Ⓑ A picture of animals hibernating
Ⓒ A diagram of the process leaves go through when changing color
Ⓓ A diagram explaining when leaves change color around the world

4. **A naturalist is presenting this information to a class of students. Which visual aid could she bring to help students understand the information in the passage?** (RI.7.7)

Ⓐ A picture of leaves that have changed color
Ⓑ A pile of leaves of different colors
Ⓒ A photograph of a pile of leaves
Ⓓ A diagram explaining the process

5. **For the information in this selection to be considered reliable, it would need to be written by....** (RI.7.8)

Ⓐ a journalist.
Ⓑ a student.
Ⓒ a scientist.
Ⓓ an environmental activist.

History of Olympics
From *Ancient Olympics Guide*

Even though the modern Olympic Games are held every four years, they bear little resemblance to the athletic contests held at Olympia in Greece in ancient times.

The games were open to competitors from all Greece, and the contests included chariot racing, horse racing, running, wrestling, boxing, and the pentathlon, a contest involving jumping, quoit- throwing, javelin throwing, running and wrestling.

Scholars date the earliest contests at 776 B.C., more than two and a half thousand years ago. The first trophies that were won consisted not of gold medals and cups but of simple crowns of olive leaves. Women and slaves were admitted neither as contestants nor as spectators. The classical games ceased to be held probably about A.D.393.

Much of the credit for the revival of the Games held at Athens in 1896 goes to Baron Pierre de Coubertin, a French classical scholar, who greatly admired the sporting ideals of the ancient Greeks. As an educationist and lover of amateurism he looked upon physical exercise as an essential feature of balanced education. Forty-two events were contested and new disciplines such as cycling, hurdling, the high jump, shooting and gymnastics were introduced.

One of the most popular events of the modern Olympics is marathon. This very tiring twenty-six mile foot race over an open course is the supreme test of the runners' endurance. The marathon was not a part of the ancient Olympics although it originated in Greece.

And, finally a more recent development in the Olympics is the introduction of the winter games, which were started in 1924. They are held separately from the summer games but in the same year. The winter Olympics provide competition in skiing, speed and figure skating, ice hockey, and rifle shooting. Such cold weather sports could never have developed in the warm climate of Greece.

1. Choose a suitable alternate title for this passage.   (RI.7.2)

Ⓐ The Winter Sports
Ⓑ The Games' Growth
Ⓒ How the Olympics Evolved
Ⓓ Popular Sports

2. The History Channel is making a documentary based on this passage. What would be most helpful for them to include?   (RI.7.7)

Ⓐ Footage from recent Olympic games
Ⓑ Video of the original Olympic games
Ⓒ Images showing the different Olympic sports from the beginning until now.
Ⓓ Interviews with current Olympic athletes

3. A gym teacher wants students to understand this passage better. What can the teacher do to make this passage more interactive?   (RI.7.7)

Ⓐ Play a video about the Olympics
Ⓑ Have students play some of the sports
Ⓒ Show students pictures of the Olympics
Ⓓ Bring in an Olympic athlete to talk to students

4. A news station has turned this piece into a special news report. When should they air it?   (RI.7.7)

Ⓐ Around the next summer or winter Olympic games
Ⓑ Right before the Super Bowl
Ⓒ Sometime in the summer
Ⓓ Sometime in the winter

Egyptian Pyramids

Today, we have high-tech cranes and other machines to help us create massive skyscrapers and other modern works of architecture. Still, some of the most breath taking architecture in the world, such as the ancient pyramids of Egypt, were created before those high-tech machines even existed. So how did those ancient civilizations create them?

Believe it or not, though they are one of the most studied and admired relics in history, there is no evidence to tell historians exactly how the Ancient Egyptians built the pyramids. Thus, they have been left to create their own theories as to how Egyptians created such amazing and awe-inspiring works of art.

According to one theory, the Egyptians placed logs under the large stone blocks in order to roll or transport them to the pyramid building location. Large groups of men would work to push or pull them into place (although historians also disagree on whether these men were slaves or skilled artisans). Still more, once the men moved the blocks to the pyramid location, they needed to lift them to ever-increasing heights to reach the top levels of the pyramid as it grew. Without modern cranes, many scientists have been baffled as to how they were able to do it. Some believe they used a ramp system that would allow them to roll the blocks upward around or through the pyramids; others believe they must have used a combination of pulleys and lifts. Still, most agree that once they did, they used a mixture of gravel and limestone to help fill any crevices and hold the mound together.

With such a primitive yet impressive building process, it's obvious that the pyramids must have taken a great deal of time to build. With an estimated 2 million blocks weighing an average of 2.5 million tons each, the Great Pyramid of Giza, for instance, is estimated to have taken some 20 years to build. At 481 feet tall, it held the record of tallest building for 3,800 years – not bad for a building created almost entirely by hand.

Even though scientists don't know exactly how the Egyptians did it, they do know that the method the Egyptians used to build pyramids changed over time. In the early days, the pyramids were made completely of stone, with limestone used to create the main body and higher quality limestone being used for the smooth outer casing. Later on, the pyramids were made mostly of mud brick with a limestone casing. Though they were likely much easier to build, they didn't stand up nearly as well over time, leaving archaeologists with even fewer clues about their creation.

http://en.wikipedia.org/wiki/Egyptian_pyramid_construction_techniques

1. What is the main idea of this selection?   (RI.7.2)

Ⓐ The Egyptians had a very advanced way of building the pyramids.
Ⓑ The Ancient Egyptians built the pyramids by hand.
Ⓒ To this day, historians are not entirely sure how the Egyptians built the pyramids.

2. **This passage is being displayed as part of a museum exhibit. What would it most likely be accompanied by?**   (RI.7.7)

Ⓐ Pictures of modern-day construction trucks
Ⓑ Pictures of Egyptians building the pyramids
Ⓒ Relics from Ancient Egypt
Ⓓ Items from Egyptian kings

3. **If creating a documentary based on this passage, what would the director most likely use in the opening sequence related to the opening of the passage?**   (RI.7.7)

Ⓐ Pictures of modern-day skyscrapers
Ⓑ Pictures of the pyramids
Ⓒ Pictures of Egyptian kings
Ⓓ Pictures of modern-day houses

4. **If this passage was turned into a play, what would it most likely be about?**   (RI.7.7)

Ⓐ A specific modern-day construction worker
Ⓑ A factual account of how pyramids were built
Ⓒ A specific pyramid-builder or group of pyramids
Ⓓ An interpretive dance of the building of pyramids

5. **Who could verify whether or not the information in this selection is accurate?**   (RI.7.8)

Ⓐ by interviewing the author of the essay
Ⓑ by reading an encyclopedia entry on the Egyptian pyramids
Ⓒ by talking with an Egyptian historian
Ⓓ by going to Egypt

The Great Round World and What's Going On In It
magazine article Anonymous author

The Moving Houses

Did you ever see a house move?

If you have not, you have missed a very funny sight.

Imagine driving along a country road, and meeting a three-story house making a journey along the highway to new quarters.

There is a good deal of this to be seen just now at Katonah, New York.

A year or so ago the Croton water-shed water, which is in use in New York City, was found to be impure.

A commission was appointed to go and examine the Croton Water-Shed. This meant that they were to examine the little streams, and brooks, and rivers, and lakes, which supplied the water to our aqueduct, and see what the trouble was.

They found that along the banks of these streams and lakes, in villages and out in the country, a great many dwelling-houses and shanties had been built, the occupants of which were in the habit of throwing all sorts of rubbish into the water, making it unfit for drinking.

In consequence of this, all of the houses were ordered to be torn down or moved away, and one small village of shanties was destroyed. Among others, the inhabitants of Katonah were ordered to move, that the banks of the stream might be cleared of dwellings.

Katonah has a railroad depot, and a post office, and thinks a good deal of itself.
When the Water-Shed Commission said that it must move or be destroyed, Katonah gathered its residents together, and decided that rather than be wiped off the face of the map, it would pick up its houses and move itself.

So a new Katonah was established, about a quarter of a mile away from the old one, and just outside the Water-Shed on which it was forbidden to build, for fear of spoiling the water for New York.
For several months past there has been a procession of houses moving from old Katonah to new.

http://www.gutenberg.org/files/15326/15326.txt

60

1. What is the main idea of this article?   (RI.7.2)

Ⓐ The water in Kantonah is polluted.
Ⓑ Many people are moving their homes because the water in Kantonah is polluted.
Ⓒ Everyone should have the experience of seeing a house being moved.
Ⓓ The people of Kantonah are angry because of the quality of their drinking water.

2. When water is described as impure, it can be assumed that...   (RI.7.4)

Ⓐ it is brown-colored.
Ⓑ it is unsafe to drink.
Ⓒ it is coming from a polluted river.
Ⓓ it is from a stream.

3. What is the author's point of view in this article?   (RI.7.6)

Ⓐ The people of Kantonah were silly to move their homes.
Ⓑ Houses should be moved regardless of the circumstances.
Ⓒ The Kantonah residents were trying to maintain control by choosing when and where they moved them.
Ⓓ The Kantonah government should pay to move people's homes.

4. Which statement from this article contains an opinion?   (RI.7.8)

Ⓐ Katonah has a railroad depot, and a post-office.
Ⓑ When the Water-Shed Commission said that it must move or be destroyed, Katonah gathered its residents together, and decided that rather than be wiped off the face of the map, it would pick up its houses and move itself.
Ⓒ Did you ever see a house move? If you have not, you have missed a very funny sight.
Ⓓ A year or so ago the Croton water-shed water, which is in use in New York City, was found to be impure.

The Great Round World and What's Going On In It
magazine article Anonymous author

Employer and Employee Predicaments

News comes from Hamburg that the strike of the dock laborers is over.

The strikers have been beaten because of their lack of money.

In No. 7 of The Great Round World you will find an account of the strike, and if you will also refer to No. 10, you will see that it was thought that the strikers could not hold out very much longer.

The money the strikers expected to receive from other labor unions to help them was so slow in coming that the men and their families were in want, and no man is likely to stand out for the benefit of others when his own children are suffering from cold and hunger.

The men have gone back to their old employers and asked for work. The pity of it all is, however, that during the strike others have been taken on in their places, and the employers have now no work to give them.

After holding out since the end of October, and refusing the masters' offer to give them $1.10 a day, and let all future troubles be settled by arbitration, the strikers have had to give in without gaining a single point. It is very sad.

1. What is this short article mostly about?   (RI.7.2)

Ⓐ Where to find more information about the Hamburg workers' strike
Ⓑ The end result of the Hamburg workers' strike
Ⓒ The causes of the Hamburg workers' strike
Ⓓ The Hamburg unions

2. What does a strike mean in reference to workers?   (RI.7.4)

Ⓐ A place where people in Hamburg work
Ⓑ A protest where workers refuse to go to work until their needs are met
Ⓒ A long list of people who are out of work.
Ⓓ A missed hit in baseball

3. Who would the author of this article be most likely to support?   (RI.7.6)

Ⓐ The business owners of Hamburg
Ⓑ The workers who were on strike
Ⓒ The workers who refused to strike

4. According to this selection, if readers want to gather more information to determine whether or not the labor strike should have taken place, where should they look?

(RI.7.8)

Ⓐ In newspapers from Hamburg
Ⓑ In past issues of the magazine this article was published in
Ⓒ In an encyclopedia
Ⓓ In other magazines

NOTES

Baseball Card Collecting

Looking for a new hobby? Do you like baseball? If you answered "yes" to these two questions baseball card collecting might be a fun pastime for you to begin! Ever since candy and gum manufacturers started putting cards with pictures of popular baseball players into the packages in the 1800's to encourage young people to buy their sweets, kids have been collecting baseball cards. Now, more than 200 years later, baseball card collecting has become a popular hobby for children and adults alike.

What You Need to Be a Baseball Card Collector

The main thing you need to start a baseball card collection is cards, of course! Baseball cards are usually sold in packs of four or more cards. Large chain stores like Walmart and Target as well as drug stores are the easiest places to find packs of baseball cards. You can also find cards at special baseball card shops. You should plan on spending around $2.99 for each pack of baseball cards you purchase. Once you've started your collection by buying packs of cards, you'll probably find that there are one or two specific cards you want that you haven't been able to get in packs. The best places to get single cards are the baseball card shows held at malls or convention centers or on the Internet. You can also trade cards with another baseball card collector. A lot of times a friend has the card you're looking for. Because you might also have a card he or she wants, trading is a great way to build the collection that you want. Plus, it doesn't cost you a cent!

As a baseball card collector you'll not only need cards, but also a place to put them. Baseball cards can become very valuable. You may get a card in a pack today that is worth ten or twenty times the price you paid for it years down the line. The price that you can sell a baseball card for is based on the condition that it is in. For this reason, you want to be sure to have a safe place to store your cards where they won't get damaged. There are lots of different options for storing baseball cards. If you have just a few important cards that you want to protect you can purchase sleeves to store them in. Sleeves are firm plastic wrappers that are slightly larger than a card. You simply slip the card into the opening on the sleeve and it is protected from wetness and bending. If you have several cards to store, consider buying boxes or albums. At baseball card shops, you can buy boxes that are specially designed to store baseball cards. For serious baseball card collectors with very valuable cards, cases that lock are the ideal spot to store your cards.

Once you've collected cards for a while you'll want a way to keep track of what cards you have in your collection. Those with small collections can use a notebook where they write down the players' names and dates of the cards they have. For those with larger collections, the computer is best place to keep track of their collections. While you can create your own database of cards using a software program on your computer, there are also special baseball card software programs that make it much easier. Beckett, the company that publishes a most popular guide to baseball card values, sells a computer program with the names of cards already loaded into it. You simply need to go in and click on the names of cards to record those that are part of your collection.

Types of Baseball Cards You Can Collect

There are four main companies that produce baseball cards: Topps, Upper Deck, Fleer and Donruss/ Playoff. The most popular and easiest cards to find in stores are those made by Topps and Upper Deck. Each of these companies sells sets of cards. You can either purchase a full set from a baseball card store or show or you can put together a set by buying enough packs of cards to collect each card in the set. The basic set put out each year by each company is made up of 500 or more cards. Cards feature posed pictures of Major League Baseball players as well as action shots. Within the basic set, there are several subsets that each has a special theme. For example, a card set might have a special subset of homerun heroes within the larger basic set they sell that year. If you buy individual packs of baseball cards to build your set you'll have a chance at getting insert cards. These are special cards that are printed in limited quantities and are inserted into packs. Insert cards are usually worth more money than basic cards because there are fewer of them produced each year.

For serious baseball collectors there are premium and specialty cards available. Premium cards come in sets and are printed by the main baseball card companies. These cards are more expensive, but feature extra perks. For example, parallel sets of premium cards are the same as the basic set, but are fancier. They might have bolder colors or special borders. In addition to premium sets, serious baseball card collectors like to collect rookie cards. A rookie card is a player's first baseball card. The year that the player is placed on a team's roster he becomes a rookie. Rookie cards become very valuable when the player goes on to have a successful career. Autographed baseball cards are another great find for devoted baseball card collectors. There are two types of autographed cards: those with autographs signed on the actual card and those with autographs cut from other sources that are glued onto the card. This second type are known as cut autos. Cut autos are usually created for players who are no longer living.

A new type of baseball cards has just come out in the last few years and may totally change card collecting in the future. Digital baseball cards are now available. These cards don't come printed on paper like traditional baseball cards. Instead, they are purchased and stored on the Internet. One of the major companies, Topps, has already had great success with their line of computer-based cards called eTopps.

Whatever type of cards you choose to collect, you're sure to find hours of enjoyment in with your new hobby.

http://en.wikibooks.org/wiki/Cultural_Anthropology/Print_version'

1. **What message does the author want the reader to walk away from the second paragraph?** (RI.7.2)

  Ⓐ A new baseball card collector should plan on having lots of money and time to start his collection.
  Ⓑ A new baseball card collector must be very organized.
  Ⓒ Baseball card collecting is easy and inexpensive.
  Ⓓ The best way to get baseball cards is to trade them.

2. **If you wanted to find information about how to start a baseball card collection, which section of this selection would you want to read?** (RI.7.5)

  Ⓐ what you need to be a baseball card collector
  Ⓑ types of baseball cards you can collect
  Ⓒ what companies make baseball cards
  Ⓓ looking for a new hobby

3. **Based on first paragraph, which statement describes the author's view of baseball card collecting?** (RI.7.6)

  Ⓐ The author thinks baseball card collecting is an expensive hobby.
  Ⓑ The author thinks baseball card collecting is a worthwhile hobby.
  Ⓒ The author thinks everyone in the world should become a baseball card collector.
  Ⓓ Baseball card collecting leads people to eat too much candy.

From ***The Great Round World and What's Going On In It*** magazine

The Czar of Russia

The Czar of Russia is quite ill, and everyone feels sorry that he should be sick now, when his advice and assistance are so badly needed to settle the worrying Turkish question, which has so troubled Europe.

The young Czar Nicholas, who was crowned with so much pomp and glory at Moscow last August, seems unable to carry on the government of Russia.

Many people say he is too weak to govern, and that there are going to be troubles and revolts in Russia.

The truth of the matter seems to be, that the young Czar is a gentle, kind-hearted man, who will not govern Russia in the stern, cruel way that his forefathers have done, and who is therefore thought to be weak and incapable.

While he is making a part of his people love him for his goodness, by far the larger half, who have, under the old rule, been able to make money and gain great power, are furious against him.

Poor young Nicholas is not only hated by the people who were most friendly to his father, but by the Nihilists, who look upon him as their natural enemy, and, between the two parties, it is said that the Czar goes about in constant fear of his life.

Nicholas never wanted to be a ruler. Those who know him say that he has become grave and sad in the few months since he came to the throne.

It is said that he is of too gentle a disposition to be able to keep his ministers in order, and that they quarrel fiercely in his presence, and show very little respect for him.

According to all accounts, his health is giving way under the constant worry, and it is reported that he received a shock a few weeks ago, which so completely upset him, that it brought on his present illness.

He was walking in his gardens, and wishing to speak to one of the men who was at work, he signalled to him to come to him. The gardener, proud of his sovereign's notice, ran towards him at full speed. But a sentry, who had not noticed the Czar's signal, fearing that the man was going to harm the Emperor, fired his gun at him, and he fell dead at the Czar's feet.

Nicholas was terribly overcome by the dreadful mistake.

Some people say that his present illness is due to anxiety about the Czarina, who is also ill, and again others say that the wound which Nicholas received when he was travelling in Japan is the cause.

He was struck by a crazy Japanese, and would have been killed, had not Prince George of Greece, the son of the present King of Greece, who was with him, warded off the blow. As it was, the blow was heavy enough to form a lump on the young man's skull, which has caused him great pain, and which some people declare is troubling him now.

Whatever the cause, the Czar is ill, and in no state to attend to anything but his own affairs. It is a sad pity just at this moment, when Europe needs him so badly.

1. Based on its use in this selection, what can you infer the meaning of the word czar is?

(RI.7.4)

Ⓐ Minister
Ⓑ King
Ⓒ Author
Ⓓ Mister

2. What is the author's view of Czar Nicholas?

(RI.7.6)

Ⓐ The author does not have much respect for Nicholas.
Ⓑ The author feels sympathy and pity for Nicholas.
Ⓒ The author thinks that Nicholas has no business being a czar.
Ⓓ The author thinks Russia is worse off now that Czar Nicholas is its ruler.

An Advertisement for SIMPLE LESSONS IN THE STUDY OF NATURE By I.G. OAKLEY
(from <u>The Great Round World and What's Going On In It</u> magazine)

This is a handy little book, which many a teacher who is looking for means to offer children genuine nature study may be thankful to get hold of.

Nature lessons, to be entitled to that name, must deal with what can be handled and scrutinized at leisure by the child, pulled apart, and even wasted. This can be done with the objects discussed in this book; they are under the feet of childhood—**grass, feathers, a fallen leaf, a budding twig, or twisted shel**l; <u>these things cannot be far out of the way, even within the stony limits of a city.</u>

Nor are the lessons haphazard dashes at the nearest living thing; on the contrary, they are virtually fundamental, whether with respect to their relation to some of the classified sciences, or with reference to the development of thought and power of expression in the child himself.

The illustrations are few, and scarcely more than figures; it is not meant to be a pretty picture-book, yet is most clearly and beautifully printed and arranged, for its material is to be that out of which pictures are made. It will be found full of suggestions of practical value to teachers who are carrying the miscellaneous work of ungraded schools, and who have the unspeakable privilege of dealing with their pupils untrammelled by cast-iron methods and account-keeping examination records.

Sample copy, 50 Cents, post-paid

WILLIAM BEVERLEY HARISON
3 & 5 W. 18th St. • • • New York City

1. What category do the items in bold all fit into?   (RI.7.4)

Ⓐ They are all animals.
Ⓑ They are all located in the author's backyard.
Ⓒ They are all items a child is likely to walk on when outside.
Ⓓ They are all plants.

2. Which statement about this book would the author of this ad be least likely to agree with?

(RI.7.6)

Ⓐ The book is educational.
Ⓑ The book offers kids great lessons about nature.
Ⓒ The book is like a children's picture book.
Ⓓ The book features items in nature a child would be likely to find on his or her own.

3. How could you determine whether or not the statement in underlined is true? (RI.7.8)

Ⓐ Purchase the book
Ⓑ Call the author and ask him if this statement is a fact or an opinion
Ⓒ Buy the book and follow the lessons in your own backyard
Ⓓ Buy the book and follow the lessons in several different settings

Advertisement from <u>The Great Round World and What's Going On In It</u> magazine--Anonymous author

Photographs in relief.

A new plan in regard to photographs has been invented.

It is to take a photograph, similar to the one that is to be embossed, and, after cutting it in a certain way, press the portions outward that it is desired shall stand in relief.

An open mask of the same shape as the photograph is then used, and the two photographs are dampened and pressed tightly together until the face and figure stand out from the card, and the picture looks as if it had been carved in wood.

This is a very ingenious invention, but the work is very difficult, and can only be done by people who are regularly trained to do it.

1. What is the meaning of relief as it is used in this selection?   (RI.7.4)

Ⓐ To feel as if a weight has been taken off your shoulders
Ⓑ Engraved
Ⓒ Sticking outward from the paper; embossed
Ⓓ Sunk into the paper

2. How does the author feel about this new invention?   (RI.7.6)

Ⓐ He thinks it will be too difficult to use.
Ⓑ It will cause less people to visit photographers.
Ⓒ He thinks this is an incredible invention.
Ⓓ It's too much like the embosser.

Bushmen

With so much technology around us each day, it is hard to imagine that anyone in the world would live without television, let alone a cell phone or radio. Still, there are a few cultures that maintain an extremely primitive lifestyle, nearly untouched by the modern world. One of those is commonly known as the Bushmen of Kalahari.

The Bushmen, also known as the "Basarwa" or "San" are found throughout southern Africa in regions of the Kalahari Desert. Nomadic hunters and gatherers by nature, they roam the region living in small kinship groups and, relatively isolated from the rest of society, have developed an extremely unique culture not otherwise seen or understood by modern man.

Unlike English, which is built on a complex system of sounds and letters, the Bushmen speak an extremely unique language made exclusively of clicking sounds. The sounds are created with a sucking action from the tongue, and even the click language itself can vary widely from tribe to tribe, making it extremely difficult to communicate with non-Bush people.

In addition to language, the Bushmen have a very different way of living. Similar to Eskimos, groups of Bushmen will live in "kinship" societies. Led by their elders, they travel together, with women in the group gathering food while men hunt for it. Children, on the other hand, have no duties other than playing. In fact, leisure is an extremely important part of the Bushmen society. Dance, music and humor are essential, with a focus on family rather than technology or development. Because of this, some people associate the Bush culture with a backward kind of living or low status.

Because of the increased speed of advancement and urban development, the Bushmen culture is in danger. Some have already been forced to switch from hunting to farming due to modernization programs in their countries. Others have been forced to move to certain areas of their countries so that modernization can continue to occur there. With so much development, it's clear that though the Bushmen culture is very rich, it is also in danger of extinction. It is unclear how long the Bush culture will continue.

http://en.wikibooks.org/wiki/Cultural_Anthropology/Print_version'

1. How are the paragraphs in this selection organized?   (RI.7.5)

Ⓐ by topic
Ⓑ from broad ideas to narrow ideas
Ⓒ chronologically
Ⓓ compare and contrast

2. Based on the passage, what is the best meaning of primitive?   (L.7.6)

- Ⓐ New and modern
- Ⓑ Not sophisticated or developed
- Ⓒ Cultural traits or traditions
- Ⓓ Languages unlike English

3. The passage describes kinship societies. If the word "kin" means "family or relations," then kinship societies are most likely...   (L.7.6)

- Ⓐ Groups of individuals who came together from different tribes
- Ⓑ Groups of individuals from the same family
- Ⓒ Groups of individuals who are married
- Ⓓ Groups of individuals who follow one leader

4. Based on the passage, what is the meaning of the word modernization?   (L.7.6)

- Ⓐ Keeping traditional practices and traditions
- Ⓑ Bringing computers and other cutting-edge technology
- Ⓒ Incorporating new practices and ideas
- Ⓓ Speaking a new language, such as English

NOTES

The Great Round World and What's Going On In It
magazine article Anonymous author

Brave Heart - Blondin

Blondin, the celebrated tight-rope walker, has just died in London, at the age of seventy-three.

The performance which made him famous was the crossing of Niagara Falls on the tight-rope.

Blondin was a Frenchman, his father having been one of Napoleon's soldiers.

A story is told of him that when he was five years old he saw an acrobat performing on a tight-rope.

He was so pleased with what he saw, that when he got home he stretched a rope between two posts, and, as soon as his mother was out of the way, took his father's fishing-rod, and, using it as a balancing pole, made his first appearance as a tight-rope walker.

He was trained for an acrobat and tight-rope walking, and came to this country with a troupe of pantomimes.

While here he visited Niagara Falls, and the idea at once struck him that, if he dared to cross those terrible waters on a rope, his fortune would be made. He made up his mind to try it, and stayed in the village of Niagara for weeks, until he had learned just how it would be possible for him to perform the feat.

Then he set about getting the scheme well-advertised, and securing plenty of money for himself if he succeeded in accomplishing it.

On August 17th, 1859, he made the trip across the Falls in the presence of 50,000 spectators.

His rope was 175 feet above the waters.

He was not satisfied with merely walking across; he crossed again blindfolded, and then carrying a man on his back, and once again wheeling a barrow before him.

In the summer of 1860 he crossed once more in the presence of the Prince of Wales, and carried a man on his back, whom he set down on the rope six times, while he rested.

1. How is this selection organized?   (RI.7.5)

Ⓐ Chronological Order
Ⓑ Order of Importance
Ⓒ Causes and Effects
Ⓓ Comparison-Contrast

2. Which of the following does the author express in this article?   (RI.7.8)

Ⓐ His opinions about Blondin
Ⓑ Factual information about Blondin
Ⓒ Both his opinions of Blondin and factual information
Ⓓ Blondin's input

Advertisement from <u>The Great Round World and What's Going On In It</u> magazine--Anonymous author

FOUR FAMOUS BOOKS

Every boy and girl is interested in what is going on about them. The authors of this series have gathered together the most interesting kind of information, and have told it in a most entertaining way.

Copies will be sent post-paid to any address upon receipt of price named.

1. Foods and Beverages, by E.A. Beal, M.D. Contains reading lessons on the various kinds of Foods and their hygienic values; on Grains, Fruits, and useful Plants, with elementary botanical instruction relating thereto; and on other common subjects of interest and importance to all, old and young. 281 pages. Cloth, 60 cents.

2. Every-Day Occupations, by H. Warren Clifford, S.D. Quantities of useful facts entertainingly told, relating to work and workers. How Leather is Tanned; How Silk is Made; The Mysteries of Glass-Making, of Cotton Manufacture, of Cloth-Making, of Ship and House Building; The Secrets of the Dyer's Art and the Potter's Skill—all and more are described and explained in detail with wonderful clearness. 330 pages. Cloth, 60 cents.

3. Man and Materials, by Wm. G. Parker, M.E. Shows how man has raised himself from savagery to civilization by utilizing the raw material of the earth. Brings for the first time the wonderful natural resources of the United States to the notice of American children. The progress of the Metal-Working arts simply described and very attractively illustrated. 323 pages. Cloth, 60 cents.

4. Modern Industries and Commerce, by Robert Louis, Ph.D. Treats of commerce and the different means of conveyance used in different eras. Highways, Canals. Tunnels, Railroads, and the Steam Engine are discussed in an entertaining way. Other subjects are Paper Manufacture, Newspapers, Electric Light, Atlantic Cable, the Telephone, and the principal newer commercial applications of Electricity, etc. 329 pages. Cloth, 60 cents.

1. How does the way the author has structured this advertisement help the reader understand the information in it?   (RI.7.5)

Ⓐ The headings organize the topics in the selection.
Ⓑ The book titles help the reader locate information about specific books.
Ⓒ The ad is organized from the most interesting to the least interesting book which helps the reader know which books are best to purchase.
Ⓓ The author numbers the items.

2. Which statement about the books in this advertisement would the author be least likely to agree with? (RI.7.6)

Ⓐ The books are educational for children.
Ⓑ There are interesting facts and descriptions in these books.
Ⓒ Most children would not find these books very useful.
Ⓓ Children are likely to be entertained by the information in these books.

3. Which of the following does the author express in this advertisement? (RI.7.8)

Ⓐ his opinions about the books.
Ⓑ factual information about the books
Ⓒ both factual information about the books and the author's opinion of the books
Ⓓ readers' viewpoints

Advertisement from <u>The Great Round World and What's Going On In It</u> magazine--Anonymous author

Advertisement

School and College Text-Books
AT WHOLESALE PRICES
At my New Store (FEBRUARY 1ST)
3 & 5 West 18th Street, The St. Ann Building

With the greatly increased facilities I can now offer to my customers the convenience of an assortment of text books and supplies more complete than any other in any store in this city. Books will be classified according to subject. Teachers and students are invited to call and refer to the shelves when in search of information; every convenience and assistance will be rendered them.

Reading Charts, miscellaneous Reference Charts, Maps, Globes, Blackboards, and School Supplies at net prices singly or in quantity.

All books removed from old store (more or less damaged by removal) will be closed out at low prices.

Mail orders promptly attended to
All books, etc., subject to approval
William Beverley Harrison, 3 & 5 West 18th Street
FORMERLY 59 FIFTH AVENUE

1. What is the author's point of view in this ad?   (RI.7.6)

Ⓐ His new store is even better than his old store.
Ⓑ His store has some of the books teachers and students need.
Ⓒ His books are now available by mail order.
Ⓓ His store has moved to a new location.

2. Which statement from this ad is NOT a fact?   (RI.7.8)

Ⓐ I can now offer to my customers the convenience of an assortment of text-books and supplies more complete than any other in any store in this city.
Ⓑ Teachers and students are invited to call and refer to the shelves when in search of information.
Ⓒ All books removed from old store (more or less damaged by removal) will be closed out at low prices.
Ⓓ Mail orders promptly attended to.

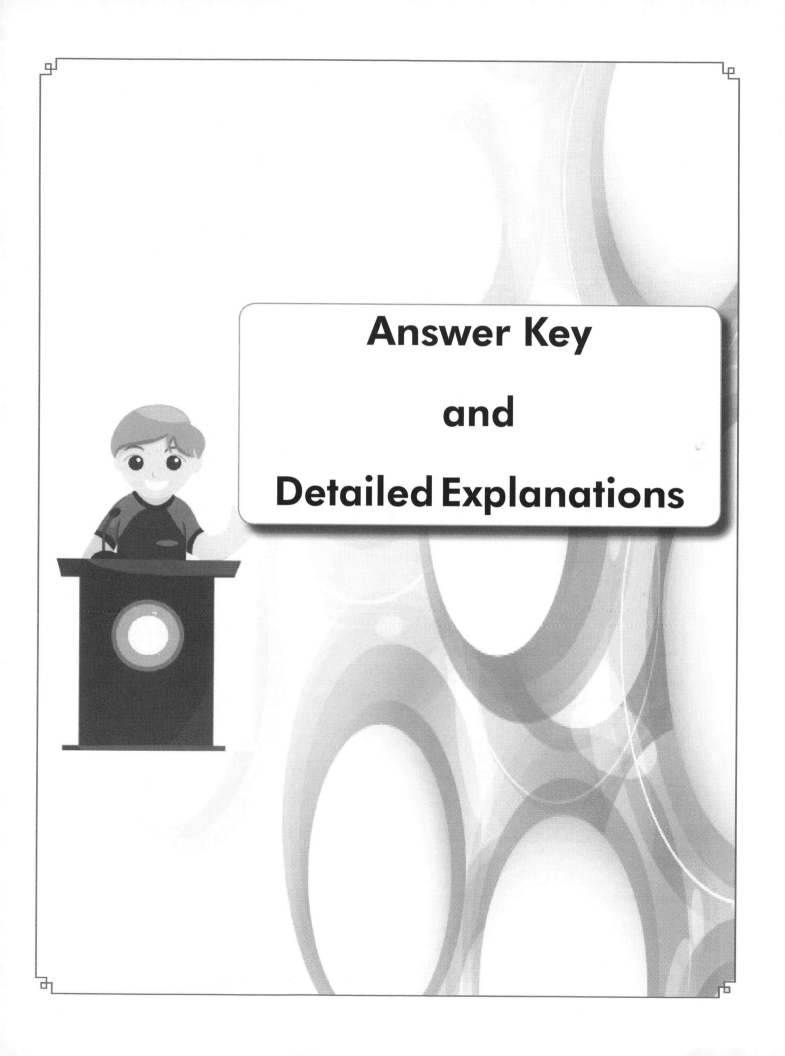

Answer Key

and

Detailed Explanations

From Scouting for Boys

Question No.	Answer	Detailed Explanations	CCSS
1	B	Answer choice two is the best answer. This answer is the best one because it shows that there were so many footprints that the policeman could not figure out exactly which prints belonged to the thief and which prints belonged to other customers. The first answer is incorrect because if the prints were marked, there would be no point in searching for the thief. The third answer choice can't be correct because the story clearly tells the reader that there are several footprints. The last answer choice does not make sense. Why would someone clean the footprints when a crime had been committed?	RL.7.1
2	B	Answer choice two is correct. The story is told from a third person's point of view. All could be "seen," but we did not know what everyone was thinking, so it is not omniscient.	RL.7.1
3	A	Answer choice one is the correct answer. The first line in the story tells the reader where it is taking place.	RL.7.3
4	A	Answer choice one is the correct answer. The shopkeeper runs out shouting for someone to stop the thief. This tells the reader he left to catch the person who stole his sugar from the store.	RL.7.3
5	B	Answer choice two is the correct answer. The policeman was able to find the "thief" by looking at the line of ants. Ants often are looking for sugar.	RL.7.3

Tryouts

Question No.	Answer	Detailed Explanations	CCSS
1	C	Answer choice three is correct. The first two choices are not mentioned in the story, so they cannot be the correct choice. The last answer choice is not the best choice. Although his mom is encouraging, she did not help him make the decision.	RL.7.1
2	D	Answer choice four is the correct answer. Sam was very concerned about what his parents would think if he missed the party. This shows he considers other's feelings and is a sign he was raised well by his parents.	RL.7.1

Question No.	Answer	Detailed Explanations	CCSS
3	A	Answer choice number one is the BEST answer of the provided choices. Sam did have trouble with tennis, but that is not the focus of the passage. Sam's mother was part of the story, but the passage was about more than just his mother. And, Sam did NOT ruin his mother's birthday.	RL.7.2
4	A	Answer choice one is the correct answer. The entire story is about the angst a young man feels when he worries about disappointing his mom. Family values and doing what is important (not missing a party) is the theme.	RL.7.2
5	C	The correct answer is choice number three. In this case the boy felt he had a problem that the only choices would hurt someone's feelings, his or his parents'. The first answer choice is a nice thought, but it isn't always true, and doesn't apply to this story since no one is coming in and out of Sam's life. The second answer choice implies that friends should not be involved in each other's lives. This is not reasonable. Sharing life's events is a major component of friendship. The last answer choice is not the best answer because some decisions should be made on one's own, with no input from others. Also, the word "always" is a hint that the choice is not a good one. Words such as "always" or "never" etcetera, usually are not the best choices because always indicates that there is no other way something can be done.	RL.7.2
6	A	Answer choice one is the correct choice. Sam's gift to his mom (according to her) was the fact the he was able to tryout for the state team. She is not focused on her birthday as much as she is on her son's achievement. She is proud of him, and wants him to do well.	RL.7.3
7	D	Answer choice four is the correct answer. Sam let the quandary bother him for a long time. He let it affect his mood and second-guess himself. Had he sought assistance earlier, he could have avoided a lot of stress.	RL.7.3
8	C	Answer choice three is the BEST answer. Choice four is possible, but the third choice best describes Sam in this passage. The first two answer choices are not reasonable for the story.	RL.7.3

Question No.	Answer	Detailed Explanations	CCSS
9	C	Answer choice three is the best answer. In the beginning of the story he is concerned about the decision he needs to make and how it will affect others. Then, after getting guidance, he is confident and happy that he gets to share his good news with his mom.	RL.7.3

Try Fairy Tales by A Brothers' Grimm outs

Question No.	Answer	Detailed Explanations	CCSS
1	C	Answer choice three is correct. The answer is in the passage and can be found in the third paragraph. The first two choices are not mentioned in the story, and although they make sense for today, this passage does not indicate that was an option. The last choice is in the story, a ride in the boat, but what is expected to cure the king is a sudden fright (something unexpected), not a ride in a boat.	RL.7.1
2	C	Answer choice number three is the correct answer. The first line of the story states that no one "except his fool" could play tricks on the king.	RL.7.3
3	D	Answer choice four is the correct answer. The fool's jokes were generally harmless, just fun. The king's joke turned out to be a sad event. So, the king likely had a different view on playing a prank on someone. He might have had a greater appreciation for his fool than he did prior to the fool dying.	RL.7.3

"The Boys and the Frogs"

Question No.	Answer	Detailed Explanations	CCSS
1	A	Answer choice one is correct. In the last part of the poem, the frog tells the boys that the rocks hit them in the head.	RL.7.1
2	D	Answer choice four is correct. Answer choices one and two are things boys might do, but the poem does not mention them doing so in this piece. Answer choice three seems possible because the frogs complain of getting hit on the head, and claiming it "'tis death to us." However, the boys are not TRYING to kill the frogs. They are throwing stones in the water.	RL.7.1
3	B	Answer choice two is correct. The frogs pleaded that the boys pay attention. This implies that the boys did not know they were hurting the frogs.	RL.7.1

From "The Dog and the Wolf" by Marmaduke Park

1	A	Answer choice one is correct. In the sixth line of the poem, there are quotation marks that indicate someone is talking. "The wolf once met...and began 'Your servant'...." section tells the reader that the wolf began speaking, therefore the best answer is choice number one.	RL.7.1
2	B	Answer choice two is the best answer. Because the dog was well fed, unlike the wolf, his master must have cared for the dog.	RL.7.1
3	C	Answer choice three is the correct answer. The wolf is hungry, while the dog is plump (fat) with living a good life free of want. The wolf is always in need of a good meal.	RL.7.1

Question No.	Answer	Detailed Explanations	CCSS
4	B	Answer choice number one is true, but it is not the best answer because it does not explain fully how the dog lives. Answer choice number two is the best answer because the dog is well fed and does not want or need anything whereas the wolf is hungry and worries about getting food. Answer choice number three is incorrect because the dog is not greedy, he doesn't take from another, he just doesn't have to worry about his needs being met. Answer choice four is not the best answer because the poem does not mention sharing.	RL.7.1

"Jane Eyre (Excerpt) by Charlotte Bronte"

1	C	Answer choice three is correct. Answer choice one is incorrect because the description of the room was meant to describe how beautiful and empty it was. There was no indication of anything haunting the room.	RL.7.1
2	B	Answer choice two is the correct answer. Answer choice one is not the best answer. Yes, the house-keeper cleans the room, but that is not a reasonable reason to avoid going in to the room. Answer choice number two is the best choice because Mrs. Reed's deceased husband has cast a spell over the room. Answer choice three is not reasonable. Even with a large home, she could go in to any room she wanted to go in to. Answer choice four is nor a reasonable answer because there is no mention of Mrs. Reed being busy or not having time to go in to the room.	RL.7.1

Question No.	Answer	Detailed Explanations	CCSS
3	D	Answer choice four is the correct answer. Answer choice number one is incorrect because other than "deceased husband" there is no mention of a Mr. Reed. Answer choice number two is not the best answer because cleaning is what the maid does, regardless of who is or is not in the room. This would not be a concern of Mrs. Reed. Answer number three is not the best answer. The room is beautifully described, but Mrs. Reed would not be concerned about messing up the furniture because she has a maid. Answer choice number four is the best answer. The fact that Mrs. Reed does not spend time in the room, as pretty as it is, only reinforces the point that she avoids the room.	RL.7.1
4	B	Answer choice two is the BEST answer. All of the other answer choices are in fact true, but the second description is the most accurate. The last answer choice does not mention the fireplace or wardrobe.	RL.7.2
5	C	Answer choice number three is the best answer. The description describes a large (size) room/home and a fire is needed to warm the place (past). Cottage is not mentioned, nor a hotel, and the fire indicates that the time is not in the future.	RL.7.3
6	A	Answer choice one is the best because it indicates that the feriplace has the only source of heat. More modern homes have furnaces. The remaining three answers describe the room and furniture. The first answer choice gives more of a an idea about how the remaining part of the home is situated. These other rooms indicate the time frame of the story. Current homes are not designed that way.	RL.7.3

""The Lament"
by Srvani"

Question No.	Answer	Detailed Explanations	CCSS
1	C	Answer choice three is correct. The quote indicates that the cabby was not paying attention, lost in thought, or asleep when the policemen called to him. It is meant to explain how the day had been slow, boring and cold, and he was somewhat startled and had a hard time getting his senses together to drive the policeman.	RL.7.1
2	A	Answer choice one is the correct answer. The cab driver indicates that his son was ill and then died. The story describes him sitting very still and somewhat dazed.	RL.7.3
3	B	Answer choice number two is the correct answer. The cab driver's son died, and due to that he was grief stricken and sad. He was confused and not sure where to go with the policeman. He was sad (lamented) about the death of his child.	RL.7.3
4	C	Answer choice three is the correct answer. Snow is not common everywhere, but where it does on a regular basis, it is a winter form of precipitation.	RL.7.3
5	A	Correct answer is the first choice. The other three answers are too general to make a determination of setting. However, the story first states the name of the cab driver, and it is a Russian name.	RL.7.3

""Bruno the Bear"
Excerpt from The Bond of Love"

Question No.	Answer	Detailed Explanations	CCSS
1	D	Answer choice four is correct. The bear behaved very differently when he went to the zoo. He would not eat and he lost weight. He was a happy bear before going to the zoo. His changed behavior was a clue that he was depressed.	RL.7.1
2	B	Answer choice two is the correct answer. The bear would not eat, and he was getting too thin. Then the wife came to see him, and he ate again.	RL.7.2
3	B	Answer choice two is the correct answer. The bear and the wife were so close that both of them were not happy/healthy when they were separated.	RL.7.2
4	B	Answer choice number two is the best answer. The story says "one day an accident befell him." This means Bruno made a mistake, or had something happened to him. In this case, he ate poison intended for rats.	RL.7.3
5	B	Answer choice two is the correct answer. The passage states, "But because of the neighborhoods' and our renters' children, poor Bruno, had to be kept chained most of the time." explains why the answer is the correct answer.	RL.7.3
6	B	Answer choice two is the best answer. Central in this case means center or main. The question asks about what is the main point of this story. This portion tells of the pet accidentally eating rat poison and nearly dying before the vet could get him the antidote shot.	RI.7.2
7	C	Answer choice number three is the best answer. All three answer choices, except the third, are true about the substance. All three are mentioned in the passage. The best answer is the substance is safe for animals. This cannot be true because it is intended to get rid of rodents and it made Bruno very ill.	RI.7.4

Best Friends to Boyfriend/Girlfriend

Question No.	Answer	Detailed Explanations	CCSS
1	A	Answer choice one is correct. They were very good friends/best friends. The passage explains their interactions with each other, indicating they were more than acquaintances or neighbors.	RL.7.1
2	D	Answer choice four is the best answer. Playing a sport or any extra-curricular activity takes up time. Practices and games take hours after school, so the answer is that the two kids could not spend as much time together as they usually did.	RL.7.3
3	A	Answer choice one is the best answer. The principal's office is usually a place students go when there is behavior issues. So, if Julie saw Max there she might assume he was in trouble, and that would support her idea that he had changed and was not the same friend she'd had. They likely would not have reconciled.	RL.7.3
4	D	Answer choice number four is the best answer. All three of the other choices in the passage are mentioned as being things causing Max stress.	RL.7.3
5	C	Answer choice number three is the answer. The other three options are mentioned in the story. There is no discussion of Max's appearance.	RL.7.3
6	C	Answer choice three is the correct answer. Max and Julie are the only two that talk. There is casual mention of the counselor at the end, but he/she is not a major part of the story.	RL.7.3

"THE OLD MAN AND THE DEVILS - A Gaelic Folk Tale (Ed. Kate Douglas Wiggin)"

Question No.	Answer	Detailed Explanations	CCSS
1	C	Answer choice three is correct. All answer choices apply somewhere in the passage. However, the third answer choice is the best summary of the second paragraph.	RL.7.2
2	C	Answer one is not the best choice. Even though the first old man danced without be self-conscious, this is not the main point of the story. Answer two is not the best choice because the old men did not negotiate with the Devil, he was offered without asking for anything. Answer three is the best choice. The first man benefitted from his time in the woods. He did not ask for the lump to be removed nor did he expect something good to happen. He was happily participating and because of this he was blessed to have the lump removed. Changing his appearance helped the first old man, but did not help the second one (had a lump added), so changing appearance does not bring someone ONLY misery.	RL.7.2
3	A	Answer choice one is the correct choice. The first man came back to the village with no lump where he previously had one. After some time another man went to the tree. It is a logical conclusion to believe that the second man was attempting to get the same help the first man did. That is the only "real" reason he'd go in to the trees.	RL.7.3

MY SHADOW by Robert Louis Stevenson

Question No.	Answer	Detailed Explanations	CCSS
1	A	The first answer choice is the best answer. The little boy is enjoying watching his shadow as he walks, skips and plays. The boy is referring to his shadow as if it is another person, but we know that it is not. The sun and the time of day affect how one sees his shadow, and this poem is hinting at that. Answer choice number three is similar to one, but the tone of the poem does not indicate confusion (which has a negative connotation), but just of fun.	RL.7.2
2	B	Answer choice three is the best answer. The little boy is the narrator of the story, and this innocence of not understanding the shadow completely adds to the mood of this poem. The main character (the boy) adds to the meaning/feeling of the poem because he is young, and everyone can relate to watching and playing with their shadow.	RL.7.3

THE WONDERFUL HAIR by A. H. Wraitslaw

1	D	Answer choice four is the best answer. To summarize something, all the information has to be included (minus small details), so the last answer is the most accurate of what is in the passage.	RL.7.2
2	B	Answer choice number one is not the best answer. Obviously it is wrong for a parent to want to hurt their children, but in THIS story, there was no indication that anyone was worried about this. Answer choice two is the best answer because the family was indeed benefited by the father's actions. Answer choice three is not the best answer because this story did not mention protecting the children, only providing food for them. Answer choice four is not the best answer because the father is the main character in the story. Without him, there is no story, so he DID have influence on the plot.	RL.7.2

Question No.	Answer	Detailed Explanations	CCSS
3	B	Answer choice two is the correct answer. In the first line of the second paragraph it states "just as the boy told him" this hints to the reader that the boy knows more than others in the story. His foreshadowing is important, and that makes the boy important in the story.	RL.7.3
4	C	Answer choice three is the best answer. Regardless where a family lives, the number of children does not affect that.	RL.7.3
5	B	Answer choice two is the best answer. "Thus the man became rich and lived on with his wife and children. And that child, that came to him in his sleep, was an angel sent by the Lord God, whose will it was to aid the poor man, and to reveal secrets which had not been revealed till then." describes a happy, relieved, and JOYFUL feeling. There is no anger, or confusion in this passage's end, nor any seriousness.	RL.7.4
6	C	Answer choice three is the best answer. The dream predicted what the man should do, and when he did this, his life improved.	RL.7.7

"The Smith and the Fairies": A Gaelic Folk Tale (Ed. Kate Douglas Wiggin)

1	C	Answer choice three is correct. The paragraph explains how the boy returns, stays silent for a year and then suddenly becomes alert and speaks again. He watches his father making a sword and feels his father is not making it correctly, and this causes him to return to talking and working.	RL.7.2
2	C	Answer choice number three is the correct answer. Making swords, fairies, and blacksmiths, indicate a time other than present day. People have been carrying Bibles and will continue to carry them. This has no bearing on time or setting.	RL.7.3
3	A	Answer choice one is the correct answer. The boy was very serious and quiet. He hardly spoke or did anything.	RL.7.7

"HOW WISDOM BECAME THE PROPERTY OF THE HUMAN RACE (West African Folktale)"

Question No.	Answer	Detailed Explanations	CCSS
1	C	Answer choice number three is the correct answer. The paragraph states that the father was offended and he set out to punish the men. He does so by hiding his wisdom from them.	RL.7.2
2	B	Answer choice number two is the correct answer. His father was trying to keep the wisdom from everyone but himself. His son followed him out of the village and watched Kewku Tsin try to climb a tree to keep wisdom away from everyone. His son saw a solution that his father did not causing the father to realize he did NOT have all the wisdom. This angered him.	RL.7.2
3	C	Answer choice three is the correct answer. The climax of a story is the changing point. This is the point that all the mystery or energy builds to. This is where the major character (protagonist) makes a decision that changes the direction of the story.	RL.7.3

""The Land of Nod" by Robert Louis Stevenson"

1	B	Answer choice one is the best choice. In this answer choice the word "nod" refers to moving one's head. In the story it is about going to sleep/dreaming (nodding off to sleep). Answer choice two is the best selection. The poem describes different places he has to go, alone, while dreaming. Also, he cannot find those places by day (when he is awake), nor can he quite remember the music (what happened in the dreams). Answer choice three might be true, but it is not the best answer. Not everything mentioned in the Land of Nod was exciting. The last answer choice is not the best answer because the poem does not indicate that the person can control where he visits.	RL.7.2
2	B	Answer choice two is the correct answer. "Nod" represents sleep (nodding off), so it implies that the person in the poem is dreaming in his sleep.	RL.7.3

The Two Melons A Chinese Folk Tale
(Ed. Kate Douglas Wiggin)

Question No.	Answer	Detailed Explanations	CCSS
1	B	Answer choice two is the best answer. The passage discusses washing clothes by a river and not being able to pay debts (money owed). This tells the reader what the time and place of the story.	RL.7.3
2	B	Answer choice two is the best answer. One woman is decent and good, the other woman only does things to benefit herself. The last answer choice is true, but it is not as good a characterization as the second choice.	RL.7.7
3	C	Answer choice three is the correct answer. The women had different attitudes towards life. Thus, the difference would not exist regardless of the order of the events.	RL.7.7

""Base Details"
by Siegfried Sassoon"

1	D	Answer choice four is the best answer. The line "speed glum heroes up the line" tells the reader that the narrator feels that the major is not considerate of the enlisted men he is charge of. The comment about being "out of breath" hints that the man is overweight, likely not a trait the younger men have.	RL.7.4
2	C	Answer choice two is the best answer. Guzzling and gulping are words that hint at greed. Also, the "best hotel" is annoying to the narrator when young men are at war on the front lines.	RL.7.4
3	B	All other answers could be inferred by the poem.	RL.7.7

From Guiseppi Verdi by Thomas Trapper

Question No.	Answer	Detailed Explanations	CCSS
1	B	Answer choice two is correct. Choice one describes how Verdi felt about the organ and man in town, and choices three and four talk about the spinet being fixed. Only choice two references how much he enjoyed practicing – so much so that he wore it out.	RI.7.1
2	A	Answer choice one is the best answer. All choices are basically correct, but the first one is the best for the passage. He was from Italy, he did play the spinet every day and probably wore it out sooner than most. But, the point of the passage is to tell the reader that the young boy loved his music and was committed to playing every day.	RI.7.2
3	A	Answer choice one is the best selection. The passaged says spinet, like a small piano. This indicates the instrument is like a piano. The passage implies the story takes place prior to electricity being common, so choice four is incorrect. Trumpet and violin are instruments, but not like an organ or piano.	RI.7.4
4	A	Answer choice number one is the best one. The other three answers are not positive or encouraging. The first choice is positive of Verdi.	RI.7.6
5	B	Answer choice two is the correct answer. Since plays normally tell stories, this passage could easily inspire a play about Verdi's childhood. A news story is not likely because this passage is from the past, a song would be awkward, and the narrative format doesn't really fit a slideshow.	RI.7.7

Skunk Chow

Question No.	Answer	Detailed Explanations	CCSS
1	D	The answer choice four is correct. The other choices talk about what skunks eat, but choice four specifically discusses how much they eat.	RI.7.1
2	C	The answer choice three is correct. Choices one and two are not true because the author doesn't need to provide the info in choice one and does provide the info negated in choice two. Choice four is true for the passage, but does not connect with skunks being omnivores.	RI.7.1
3	C	The answer choice three is the best answer. The first line tells the reader what skunks eat, and it mentions eating fruits, veggies and other animals.	RI.7.4
4	C	Answer choice number three is the best answer. The phrase "unable to find live animals to eat," indicates that scavenger means to eat dead animals.	RI.7.4

"Fall Leaves
USDA Forest Service"

1	B	All answer choices seem to be correct, but the best answer is the second choice. The article does discuss fall weather and trees, but it does not <u>focus</u> on weather. Also, the point is not the life cycle of TREES, but the process of the leaves turning in the fall and dropping from the trees.	RI.7.2
2	A	Answer choice one is correct. A time-lapse video of the leaves changing color may be included in a documentary to help someone understand how the leaves change color. Paintings are just representations, not the real thing, animals hibernating are an example given in the text but not helpful, and subtitles wouldn't do much more than the text itself.	RI.7.7

Question No.	Answer	Detailed Explanations	CCSS
3	C	Answer choice three is correct. A diagram of the process would be most helpful. The other three could be used to make it more entertaining or to add minor details.	RI.7.7
4	B	Answer choice two is correct. While a diagram would be helpful and the picture and photograph would be interesting, letting students see and compare the leaves would be best.	RI.7.7
5	C	Answer choice three is correct. A scientist should present the information without any slant or bias to a specific belief or cause. A journalist might want to tell a story with more exciting aspects to get viewers, a student might not know enough facts and information to be completely accurate, and an activist might have a cause they want focus on, so they might not be as fair at the information as a scientist should be.	RI.7.8

"History of Olympics From Ancient Olympics Guide"

1	C	Answer choice three is the best answer. The first choice is only about winter sports. The second answer is closer to what the article is about, however the third answer is BEST. The last answer is not appropriate. Popular Sports is too broad. The article was about a specific sporting event that is extremely old, so the third answer choice is the most accurate.	RI.7.2
2	C	Answer choice three is the best answer. Choices one and four are too recent to be useful and answer choice two is not possible because video didn't exist during the original Olympics.	RI.7.7
3	B	Answer choice two is the best answer. Having students play the games will make the passage more interactive and help them understand the different sports it talks about.	RI.7.7
4	A	Answer choice one is the best answer. The piece talks about the Olympics, so they should air it near the Olympics competition so that it makes more sense.	RI.7.7

Egyptian Pyramids

Question No.	Answer	Detailed Explanations	CCSS
3	C	The last answer choice is the best choice. The passage discusses how various parts of the pyramids were possibly constructed. No one is sure exactly how they were built; they only have theories.	RI.7.2
7	B	Answer choice two is correct. The passage talks about Egyptian pyramids and how they were built, so it would best be paired with images of the building process. Answer choice three is plausible, but not directly related to building.	RI.7.7
8	A	Answer choice one is correct. The opening paragraph references some of today's breath-taking structures in the world today, so it'd make sense to open the documentary with pictures of skyscrapers. Choices two and three would come later in the documentary, while choice four is too ordinary to be included.	RI.7.7
9	C	Answer choice three is correct. Plays are usually fiction, so it would most likely focus on a specific worker or group of workers and tell their story. Choice one is likely but the pyramids wouldn't be the main focus. Choice four could be part, but not the entire thing and choice two does not fit the play genre.	RI.7.7
2	C	Answer choice three is correct. One could interview the author, but what if he/she did not research properly? Reading an encyclopedia is a good start, but the historian who specializes in Egypt would be the best source for verifying the information. Going to Egypt might be fun, but that would not necessarily tell the reader if the information in the article is factual.	RI.7.8

The Moving Houses

Question No.	Answer	Detailed Explanations	CCSS
1	B	Answer choice two is the correct answer. Answer choice one is a true statement, but it is not the complete answer for the question. Answer choice three is interesting, and the author sort of hints at this concept in the beginning of the passage, but it is not the point of the passage. The people of Katonah were upset, but they chose to move before someone forced them to move. So, they are not really angry, but more proactive.	RI.7.2
2	B	Answer choice two is the best answer. Impure means not perfect or clean. The passage mentions water being impure and then later discusses how water was unfit to drink. Therefore not safe to drink is the best choice.	RI.7.4
3	C	Answer choice three is the best answer. The residents knew they were going to have their town destroyed, so they made the decision to move themselves and maintain their town.	RI.7.6
4	C	Answer choice three is the correct answer. The word funny is not provable. What is funny to one person is not necessarily funny to another. The remaining three answer choices are facts that can easily be proven by details and information easily obtained.	RI.7.8

Employer and Employee Predicaments

1	B	Answer choice two is the best answer. The article is about strikes and unions but that is not the overall focus of the story. And the article does not really elaborate on the "why" of the strike, only the end and what happened to the men.	RI.7.2
2	B	B is the answer. A strike is a protest of workers to gain benefits from employers.	RI.7.4

Question No.	Answer	Detailed Explanations	CCSS
3	B	Answer choice number two is the best choice. The author chronicles what the striking workers did and how they felt. Then the author mentions that they worked really hard but were not successful. The author indicates he's sad for the workers lack of success.	RI.7.6
4	B	The article tells the reader where he/she can find more background information on the strike (No.'s 7 & 10); answer choice two is the correct answer. The other answer choices do not make sense. To find information on a specific event, just "other magazines" is not detailed enough to find the necessary information. Newspapers might be a good source, but since the author tells the reader where the information is, looking through old newspapers is not necessary. And an encyclopedia would not have that information recorded yet. The news is too new.	RI.7.8

Baseball Card Collecting

Question No.	Answer	Detailed Explanations	CCSS
1	C	Answer choice three is the best answer. The article explains how to get started and details the easy steps and low cost.	RI.7.2
2	A	Answer choice one is the best answer to the question. The second answer is part of the passage, but does not address the question asked. The last two answer choices are in the passage, but they are not "sections" that would answer the question.	RI.7.5
3	B	Answer choice number two is the best. The author explains his opinion of collecting cards. The tone is pleasant and explains how/why one would want to collect cards.	RI.7.6

The Czar of Russia

Question No.	Answer	Detailed Explanations	CCSS
1	B	Answer choice two is the correct answer. The word Czar is like a king. The reader knows this because the passage refers to needing the Czar for leadership and that Europe needs him.	RI.7.4
2	B	Answer choice number two is the best answer. The author describes the czar's personality and discusses what others thought of him. The author mentions the czar's gentleness and desire to not be so firm as his father, yet most of the people did not understand this, so he was not well thought of. The author feels the czar was trying to do well and was misunderstood.	RI.7.6

An Advertisement for SIMPLE LESSONS IN THE STUDY OF NATURE By I.G. OAKLEY (from The Great Round World and What's Going On In It magazine)

1	C	Answer choice number three is the best selection. The passage mentions under childhood feet which implies that these are items a child might run across while walking outside. NONE of the other three choices apply to this passage.	RI.7.4
2	A	Answer choice number one is the best choice. The article describes how the old books will be discounted and that the facilities are "greatly increased." This tells the reader that the author is pleased with his new store.	RI.7.6
3	D	Answer choice four is the correct answer. A child would need to follow directions in various places. The backyard is not varied enough. Just buying the book will not help prove the bolded portion of the information. Interviewing the author is pointless. Obviously he/she believes it will work, or they would not have included the information in the book.	RI.7.8

The Great Round World and What's Going On In It
magazine article

Question No.	Answer	Detailed Explanations	CCSS
1	C	Answer choice three is the best answer. The phrase "press the portions outward" explain that "relief" means to not be flat, but to be above the picture.	RI.7.4
2	C	Answer choice number three is the best answer. Although the author thinks that the invention is limiting due to having to know how to do the process, he does think that the invention is very good!	RI.7.6

Bushmen

1	A	Answer choice one is the best answer. Each paragraph covers a different aspect of the life of the Bushmen. Answer choice two is not at all reasonable. The passage does not narrow down to one aspect. Answer choice three is incorrect because the passage is not organized in the order something happened. Answer four is incorrect too because there is nothing to compare. This is an informative passage.	RI.7.5
2	B	Answer choice two is correct. Primitive describes something not sophisticated or developed. For example, early man is often considered primitive.	L.7.6
3	B	Answer choice two is correct. A kinship society is most likely formed with groups of individuals from the same families.	L.7.6
4	C	Answer choice three is correct. Modernization does not just involve technology (choice two), but bringing in new ideas and practices.	L.7.6

Brave Heart - Blondin

Question No.	Answer	Detailed Explanations	CCSS
1	A	Answer choice one is the correct answer. The article tells of a tight-rope walker. It chronicles a period of time in the walker's life. It is done so in the order that the events happened, thus the answer is chronological.	RI.7.5
2	B	Answer choice two is correct. The passage is factual information. Opinions of anyone are not included.	RI.7.

FOUR FAMOUS BOOKS

1	B	Answer choice two is the correct answer. There are no true headings for the advertisement (choice one), and choice three does not make sense. How can the person making the advertisement know what everybody else's interest are? The last answer choice is true, but not the best answer for the question.	RI.7.5
2	C	Answer choice three is the correct answer. The author states in the first part of the passage that children are curious and want to know things. This indicates that he believes the books listed will be interesting and useful to children.	RI.7.6
3	C	Answer choice three is the correct answer. He does not include readers' viewpoints and the other two answers are correct, but the third answer is the most correct.	RI.7.8

Advertisement

3	A	Answer choice number one is the best choice. The article describes how the old books will be discounted and that the facilities are "greatly increased." This tells the reader that the author is pleased with his new store.	RI.7.6
5	A	Answer choice one is NOT a fact. It is an opinion that this store is better than any other in the city. That cannot be proven. The other choices are in fact something that could be verified.	RI.7.8

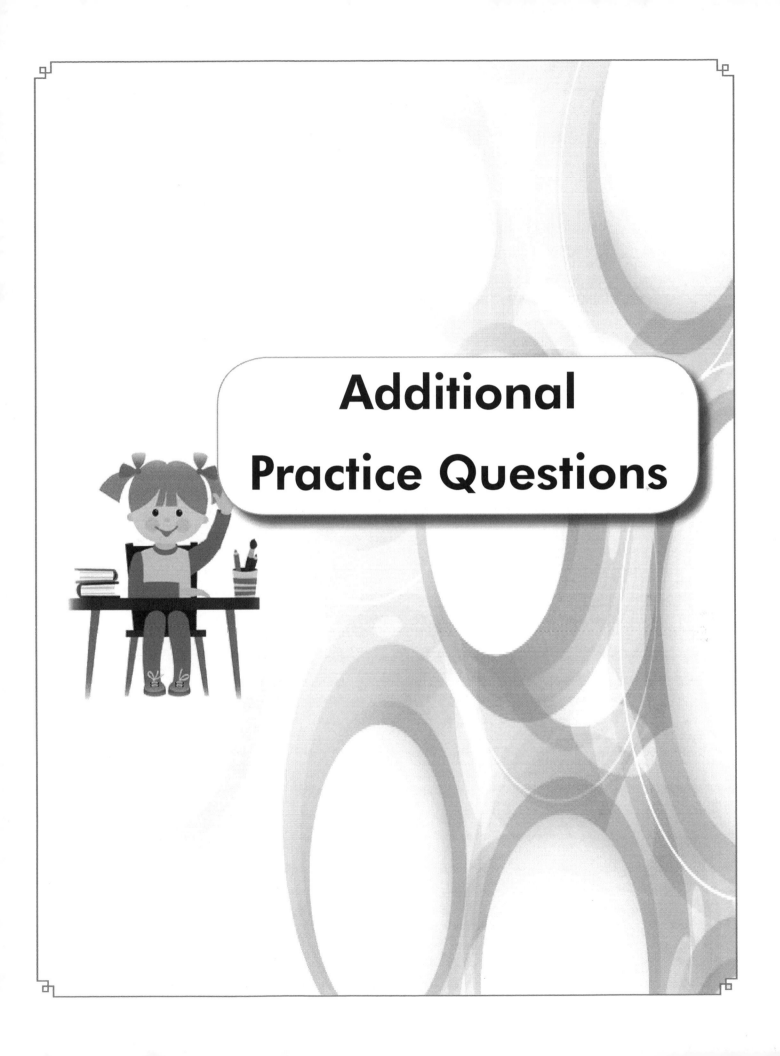

Additional Practice Questions

From "The Owl and the Pussy-Cat" by Edward Lear

The Owl and the Pussy-Cat went to sea
 In a beautiful pea-green boat,
They took some honey, and plenty of money
 Wrapped up in a five-pound note.
The Owl looked up to the stars above,
 And sang to a small guitar,
"O lovely Pussy! O Pussy, my love,
 What a beautiful Pussy you are,
   You are,
   You are!
What a beautiful Pussy you are!"
Pussy said to the Owl, "You elegant fowl!
 How charmingly sweet you sing!
O let us be married! too long we have tarried:
 But what shall we do for a ring?"
They sailed away for a year and a day,
 To the land where the Bong-tree grows,
And there in a wood a Piggy-wig stood,
 With a ring at the end of his nose,
   His nose,
   His nose,
 With a ring at the end of his nose.

1. Who provides the wedding ring for the wedding?   (RL.7.1)

Ⓐ The Owl
Ⓑ The Pussy-Cat
Ⓒ The Pig
Ⓓ The Bong-tree

From <u>The Children of France</u> by Ruth Royce

Before the "Squire's" son went away to war, the neighborhood children knew him only by sight and by hearing their parents speak of him as the son of "the richest man in Titusville," who never had done a day's work in his life.

Perhaps the parents were not quite right in this, for, even if Robert Favor had not gone out in the fields to labor, he had graduated from high school and college with high honors. He never spoke to the village children nor noticed them, and was not, as a result, very popular with the young people of his home town. The neighbors said this was all on account of his bringing up.

It was therefore a surprise to them when, at the beginning of the great war, after Germany swept over Belgium, Robert Favor hurried to Europe. It was later learned that he had joined what is known as the "Foreign Legion" of the French Army. Titusville next heard that he had been made a lieutenant for heroic conduct under fire. But Titusville did not believe it; it said no Favor ever did anything but run away in such circumstances. But they believed it when, later on, they read in the newspapers how Lieutenant Favor had sprung out of the trenches and ran to the rescue of a wounded private soldier who had lain in a shell hole in No Man's Land since the night before.

The village swelled with pride and the eyes of the children grew wide with wonder as they listened to the story of the heroism of the Squire's son. But this was as nothing to what occurred later. "Bob" Favor was brought home one day to the house on the hill, pale and weak from wounds received in battle.

Spring was at hand, and as soon as he was able, Captain Favor—you see he had again been promoted—was taken out on the lawn where, in his wheel chair he rested in the warm sunshine. The bright red top of his gray-blue cap, and the flash of the medal on his breast excited the wonder of the children, who pressed their faces against the high iron fence and gazed in awe. It was the first real hero any of them ever had seen.

Finally, chancing to look their way, the Captain smiled and waved a friendly hand. A little girl clapped her hands, others started to cheer and a little man of ten dragged an American flag from his pocket and waved it. The Captain beckoned to the children.

"Come in, folks," he called. "I wish someone to talk to me and make me laugh. Are you coming?"

They were. The children started, at first hesitatingly, then with more confidence, led by the boy with the American flag, which he was waving bravely now.

"What's your name?" demanded the Captain.

"Joe Funk, sir."

The Captain laughed. "No boy so patriotic as you are should have a name like that," he said. "We all are going to be great friends, I am sure, and when I get this leg, that a German shell nearly blew off, in working order again, we shall have some real sport and I'll teach you all how to be soldiers. Just now I cannot do much of anything."

"Yes, you can," interrupted Joe. "You can tell us how you rescued the soldier when the Germans were shooting at you and—"

"Master Joseph," answered the Captain gravely, "a real soldier never brags about himself; but what you say does give me an idea. How would you like to have me tell you about the brave little children of France?"

"Well, I'd rather hear about how you killed the Germans, lots of 'em; I want to hear about battles and dead men and—"

"We shall speak of the children first, and I will begin right now. Let me see. Ah! I have it. Sit down on the grass, all of you, and be comfortable. Be quiet until I finish the story, then ask what questions you wish. Now listen!"

2. Based on the details in this story, what do you think brought the Captain back to Titusville?

(RL.7.1)

- Ⓐ He was injured during the war and could no longer fight.
- Ⓑ He wanted to tell the people of Titusville his heroic stories.
- Ⓒ He wanted to make the people of Titusville proud of him.
- Ⓓ He wanted to work on his father's farm again.

Moral of "The Dog and the Wolf" by Marmaduke Park

Our neighbors sometimes seem to be
A vast deal better off than we;
Yet seldom 'tis they really are,
Since they have troubles too to bear,
Which, if the truth were really known,
Are quite as grievous as our own.

3. What is the best summary of the moral of this poem?

(RL.7.3)

- Ⓐ It's best to ignore those who complain.
- Ⓑ Dogs and wolves will never get along.
- Ⓒ Everyone else has problems too, that are likely to be grievous as yours.
- Ⓓ Avoid those who look down on you.

"The Origin of the Robin"
From *A Guide to Mythology* by Cornelius Mathews

An old man had an only son, named Iadilla, who had come to that age which is thought to be most proper to make the long and final fast which is to secure through life a guardian genius or spirit. The father was ambitious that his son should surpass all others in whatever was deemed wisest and greatest among his people. To accomplish his wish, he thought it necessary that the young Iadilla should fast a much longer time than any of those renowned for their power or wisdom, whose fame he coveted.

He therefore directed his son to prepare with great ceremony for the important event. After he had been several times in the sweating-lodge and bath, which were to prepare and purify him for communion with his good spirit, he ordered him to lie down upon a clean mat in a little lodge expressly provided for him. He enjoined upon him at the same time to endure his fast like a man, and promised that at the expiration of twelve days he should receive food and the blessing of his father.

The lad carefully observed the command, and lay with his face covered, calmly awaiting the approach of the spirit which was to decide his good or evil fortune for all the days of his life.

Every morning his father came to the door of the little lodge and encouraged him to persevere, dwelling at length on the vast honor and renown that must ever attend him, should he accomplish the full term of trial allotted to him.

To these glowing words of promise and glory the boy never replied, but he lay without the least sign of discontent or murmuring until the ninth day, when he addressed his father as follows:

"My father, my dreams forbode evil. May I break my fast now, and at a more favorable time make a new fast?"

The father answered:
"My son, you know not what you ask. If you get up now, all your glory will depart. Wait patiently a little longer. You have but three days more, and your term will be completed. You know it is for your own good, and I encourage you to persevere. Shall not your aged father live to see you a star among the chieftains and the beloved of battle?"

The son assented; and covering himself more closely, that he might shut out the light which prompted him to complain, he lay till the eleventh day, when he repeated his request.

The father addressed Iadilla as he had the day before, and promised that he would himself prepare his first meal, and bring it to him by the dawn of the morning.

The son moaned, and the father added:
"Will you bring shame upon your father when his sun is falling in the west?"

"I will not shame you, my father," replied Iadilla; and he lay so still and motionless that you could only know that he was living by the gentle heaving of his breast.

At the spring of day, the next morning, the father, delighted at having gained his end, prepared a repast for his son, and hastened to set it before him. On coming to the door of the little lodge, he was surprised to hear his son talking to himself. He stooped his ear to listen, and, looking through a small opening, he was yet more astonished when he beheld his son painted with vermilion over all his breast, and in the act of finishing his work by laying on the paint as far back on his shoulders as he could reach with his hands, saying at the same time, to himself:

"My father has destroyed my fortune as a man. He would not listen to my requests. He has urged me beyond my tender strength. He will be the loser. I shall be forever happy in my new state, for I have been obedient to my parent. He alone will be the sufferer, for my guardian spirit is a just one. Though not propitious to me in the manner I desired, he has shown me pity in another way—he has given me another shape; and now I must go."

At this moment the old man broke in, exclaiming:
"My son! my son! I pray you leave me not!"

But the young man, with the quickness of a bird, had flown to the top of the lodge and perched himself on the highest pole, having been changed into a beautiful robin red-breast. He looked down upon his father with pity beaming in his eyes, and addressed him as follows:

"Regret not, my father, the change you behold. I shall be happier in my present state than I could have been as a man. I shall always be the friend of men, and keep near their dwellings. I shall ever be happy and contented; and although I could not gratify your wishes as a warrior, it will be my daily aim to make you amends for it as a harbinger of peace and joy. I will cheer you by my songs, and strive to inspire in others the joy and lightsomeness of heart I feel in my present state. This will be some compensation to you for the loss of glory you expected. I am now free from the cares and pains of human life. My food is spontaneously furnished by the mountains and fields, and my pathway of life is in the bright air."

Then stretching himself on his toes, as if delighted with the gift of wings, Iadilla caroled one of his sweetest songs, and flew away into a neighboring wood.

4. What is the theme of this story?   (RL.7.2)

  Ⓐ Disobedient children will be punished.
  Ⓑ Children lead their parents to Heaven.
  Ⓒ Being obedient does not always have the intended result.
  Ⓓ Dying is honorable.

5. What message about parents is the author trying to send through this story?   (RL.7.2)

  Ⓐ Parents should listen to their children.
  Ⓑ Effective parents are strict with their children.
  Ⓒ Parents always know best.
  Ⓓ Children take their parents for granted.

Aesop in Rhyme "The Philosopher and the Acorn" by Marmaduke Park

A philosopher, proud of his wit and his reason,
Sat him under an oak in a hot summer season.
On the oak grew an acorn or two, it is said:
On the ground grew a pumpkin as big as his head.
Thought the sage, "What's the reason this oak is so strong
A few acorns to bear that are scarce an inch long;
While this poor feeble plant has a weight to sustain,
Which had much better hang on the tree, it is plain?"
But just at the time the philosopher spoke
An acorn dropp'd down on his head from the oak;
Then, said he, who just now thought his plan was so clever,
"I am glad that this was not a pumpkin, however."

6. What is the theme of this poem?   (RL.7.2)

  Ⓐ Watch out for falling objects.
  Ⓑ Just because something is small doesn't mean it isn't mighty.
  Ⓒ Don't question the way Mother Nature works.
  Ⓓ Every seed becomes a beautiful plant.

Name: _____   Date: _____

Excerpt from *The Wonderful Wizard of Oz*
L. Frank Baum

Dorothy lived in the midst of the great Kansas prairies, with Uncle Henry, who was a farmer, and Aunt Em, who was the farmer's wife. Their house was small, for the lumber to build it had to be carried by wagon many miles. There were four walls, a floor and a roof, which made one room; and this room contained a rusty looking cooking stove, a cupboard for the dishes, a table, three or four chairs, and the beds. Uncle Henry and Aunt Em had a big bed in one corner, and Dorothy a little bed in another corner. There was no garret at all, and no cellar-except a small hole, dug in the ground, called a cyclone cellar, where the family could go in case one of those great whirlwinds arose, mighty enough to crush any building in its path. It was reached by a trap-door in the middle of the floor, from which a ladder led down into the small, dark hole.

When Dorothy stood in the doorway and looked around, she could see nothing but the great gray prairie on every side. Not a tree nor a house broke the broad sweep of flat country that reached the edge of the sky in all directions. The sun had baked the plowed land into a gray mass, with little cracks running through it. Even the grass was not green, for the sun had burned the tops of the long blades until they were the same gray color to be seen everywhere. Once the house had been painted, but the sun blistered the paint and the rains washed it away, and now the house was as dull and gray as everything else.

When Aunt Em came there to live she was a young, pretty wife. The sun and wind had changed her, too. They had taken the sparkle from her eyes and left them a sober gray; they had taken the red from her cheeks and lips, and they were gray also. She was thin and gaunt, and never smiled, now. When Dorothy, who was an orphan, first came to her, Aunt Em had been so startled by the child's laughter that she would scream and press her hand upon her heart whenever Dorothy's merry voice reached her ears; and she still looked at the little girl with wonder that she could find anything to laugh at.

Uncle Henry never laughed. He worked hard from morning till night and did not know what joy was. He was gray also, from his long beard to his rough boots, and he looked stern and solemn, and rarely spoke.

It was Toto that made Dorothy laugh, and saved her from growing as gray as her other surroundings. Toto was not gray; he was a little black dog, with long, silky hair and small black eyes that twinkled merrily on either side of his funny, wee nose. Toto played all day long, and Dorothy played with him, and loved him dearly.

To-day, however, they were not playing. Uncle Henry sat upon the door-step and looked anxiously at the sky, which was even grayer than usual. Dorothy stood in the door with Toto in her arms, and looked at the sky too. Aunt Em was washing the dishes.

From the far north they heard a low wail of the wind, and Uncle Henry and Dorothy could see where the long grass bowed in waves before the coming storm. There now came a sharp whistling in the air from the south, and as they turned their eyes that way they saw ripples in the grass coming from that direction also.

Suddenly Uncle Henry stood up.
"There's a cyclone coming, Em," he called to his wife; "I'll go look after the stock." Then he ran to-ward the sheds where the cows and horses were kept.
Aunt Em dropped her work and came to the door. One glance told her of the danger close at hand.

"Quick, Dorothy!" she screamed; "run for the cellar!"

Toto jumped out of Dorothy's arms and hid under the bed, and the girl started to get him. Aunt Em, badly frightened, threw open the trap-door in the floor and climbed down the ladder into the small, dark hole. Dorothy caught Toto at last, and started to follow her aunt. When she was half way across the room there came a great shriek from the wind, and the house shook so hard that she lost her footing and sat down suddenly upon the floor.

7. **Which line or lines from this excerpt support the conclusion that this story is set in the past?**   (RL.7.3)

   Ⓐ When Dorothy stood in the doorway and looked around, she could see nothing but the great gray prairie on every side. Not a tree nor a house broke the broad sweep of flat country that reached the edge of the sky in all directions

   Ⓑ Uncle Henry never laughed. He worked hard from morning till night and did not know what joy was.

   Ⓒ Their house was small, for the lumber to build it had to be carried by wagon many miles.

   Ⓓ Once the house had been painted, but the sun blistered the paint and the rains washed it away, and now the house was as dull and gray as everything else.

NOTES

From THE HISTORY OF THE SEVEN FAMILIES OF THE LAKE PIPPLE-POPPLE. by Edward Lear

The Parrots lived upon the Soffsky-Poffsky trees, which were beautiful to behold, and covered with blue leaves; and they fed upon fruit, artichokes, and striped beetles.

The Storks walked in and out of the Lake Pipple-Popple, and ate frogs for breakfast, and buttered toast for tea; but on account of the extreme length of their legs they could not sit down, and so they walked about continually. The Geese, having webs to their feet, caught quantities of flies, which they ate for dinner.

The Owls anxiously looked after mice, which they caught, and made into sago-puddings. The Guinea Pigs toddled about the gardens, and ate lettuces and Cheshire cheese.

The Cats sate still in the sunshine, and fed upon sponge biscuits. The Fishes lived in the lake, and fed chiefly on boiled periwinkles. And all these seven families lived together in the utmost fun and felicity.

8. How do the author's descriptions of the animals' habitats affect the tone of the story?

(RL.7.4)

Ⓐ They make the animals appear hungry all the time.
Ⓑ They make the animals seem greedy.
Ⓒ They create a tone of nonsense and silliness.
Ⓓ They show how diverse the animals are.

From *The Moribund* by Guy de Maupassant

The warm autumn sun was beating down on the farmyard. Under the grass, which had been cropped close by the cows, the earth soaked by recent rains, was soft and sank in under the feet with a soggy noise, and the apple trees, loaded with apples, were dropping their pale green fruit in the dark green grass.

Four young heifers, tied in a line, were grazing and at times looking toward the house and lowing. The fowls made a colored patch on the dung-heap before the stable, scratching, moving about and cackling, while two roosters crowed continually, digging worms for their hens, whom they were calling with a loud clucking.

The wooden gate opened and a man entered. He might have been forty years old, but he looked at least sixty, wrinkled, bent, walking slowly, impeded by the weight of heavy wooden shoes full of straw. His long arms hung down on both sides of his body. When he got near the farm a yellow cur, tied at the foot of an enormous pear tree, beside a barrel which served as his kennel, began at first to wag his tail and then to bark for joy.

115

The man cried:
"Down, Finot!"
The dog was quiet.

A peasant woman came out of the house. Her large, flat, bony body was outlined under a long wool-len jacket drawn in at the waist. A gray skirt, too short, fell to the middle of her legs, which were en-cased in blue stockings. She, too, wore wooden shoes, filled with straw. The white cap, turned yellow, covered a few hairs which were plastered to the scalp, and her brown, thin, ugly, toothless face had that wild, animal expression which is often to be found on the faces of the peasants.

The man asked:
"How is he gettin' along?"

The woman answered:
"The priest said it's the end--that he will never live through the night."
Both of them went into the house.

After passing through the kitchen, they entered a low, dark room, barely lighted by one window, in front of which a piece of calico was hanging.

The big beams, turned brown with age and smoke, crossed the room from one side to the other, sup-porting the thin floor of the garret, where an army of rats ran about day and night.

The moist, lumpy earthen floor looked greasy, and, at the back of the room, the bed made an in-distinct white spot. A harsh, regular noise, a difficult, hoarse, wheezing breathing, like the gurgling of water from a broken pump, came from the darkened couch where an old man, the father of the peasant woman, was dying.

The man and the woman approached the dying man and looked at him with calm, resigned eyes. The son-in-law said:
"I guess it's all up with him this time; he will not last the night."

The woman answered:
"He's been gurglin' like that ever since midday." They were silent. The father's eyes were closed, his face was the color of the earth and so dry that it looked like wood. Through his open mouth came his harsh, rattling breath, and the gray linen sheet rose and fell with each respiration.

9. In the paragraph in bold, what is the author's tone toward the woman described?

(RL.7.4)

Ⓐ sympathy
Ⓑ repulsed
Ⓒ anger
Ⓓ longing

116

Excerpt from *Little Women*
By Louisa May Alcott

"Christmas won't be Christmas without any presents," grumbled Jo, lying on the rug.

"It's so dreadful to be poor!" sighed Meg, looking down at her old dress.

"I don't think it's fair for some girls to have plenty of pretty things, and other girls nothing at all," added little Amy, with an injured sniff.

"We've got Father and Mother, and each other," said Beth contentedly from her corner.

The four young faces on which the firelight shone brightened at the cheerful words, but darkened again as Jo said sadly, "We haven't got Father, and shall not have him for a long time." She didn't say "perhaps never," but each silently added it, thinking of Father far away, where the fighting was.

Nobody spoke for a minute; then Meg said in an altered tone, "You know the reason Mother proposed not having any presents this Christmas was because it is going to be a hard winter for everyone; and she thinks we ought not to spend money for pleasure, when our men are suffering so in the army. We can't do much, but we can make our little sacrifices, and ought to do it gladly. But I am afraid I don't." And Meg shook her head, as she thought regretfully of all the pretty things she wanted.

"But I don't think the little we should spend would do any good. We've each got a dollar, and the army wouldn't be much helped by our giving that. I agree not to expect anything from Mother or you, but I do want to buy UNDINE AND SINTRAM for myself. I've wanted it so long," said Jo, who was a bookworm.

"I planned to spend mine in new music," said Beth, with a little sigh, which no one heard but the hearth brush and kettle holder.

"I shall get a nice box of Faber's drawing pencils. I really need them," said Amy decidedly.

"Mother didn't say anything about our money, and she won't wish us to give up everything. Let's each buy what we want, and have a little fun. I'm sure we work hard enough to earn it," cried Jo, examining the heels of her shoes in a gentlemanly manner.

"I know I do--teaching those tiresome children nearly all day, when I'm longing to enjoy myself at home," began Meg, in the complaining tone again.

"You don't have half such a hard time as I do," said Jo. "How would you like to be shut up for hours with a nervous, fussy old lady, who keeps you trotting, is never satisfied, and worries you till you're ready to fly out the window or cry?"

"It's naughty to fret, but I do think washing dishes and keeping things tidy is the worst work in the world. It makes me cross, and my hands get so stiff, I can't practice well at all." And Beth looked at her rough hands with a sigh that anyone could hear that time.

"I don't believe any of you suffer as I do," cried Amy, "for you don't have to go to school with impertinent girls, who plague you if you don't know your lessons, and laugh at your dresses, and label your father if he isn't rich, and insult you when your nose isn't nice."

"If you mean libel, I'd say so, and not talk about labels, as if Papa was a pickle bottle," advised Jo, laughing.

"I know what I mean, and you needn't be satirical about it. It's proper to use good words, and improve your vocabulary," returned Amy, with dignity.

"Don't peck at one another, children. Don't you wish we had the money Papa lost when we were little, Jo? Dear me! How happy and good we'd be, if we had no worries!" said Meg, who could remember better times.

"You said the other day you thought we were a deal happier than the King children, for they were fighting and fretting all the time, in spite of their money."

"So I did, Beth. Well, I think we are. For though we do have to work, we make fun of ourselves, and are a pretty jolly set, as Jo would say."

"Jo does use such slang words!" observed Amy, with a reproving look at the long figure stretched on the rug.

Jo immediately sat up, put her hands in her pockets, and began to whistle.

"Don't, Jo. It's so boyish!"

"That's why I do it."

"I detest rude, unladylike girls!"

"I hate affected, niminy-piminy chits!"

"Birds in their little nests agree," sang Beth, the peacemaker, with such a funny face that both sharp voices softened to a laugh, and the "pecking" ended for that time.

"Really, girls, you are both to be blamed," said Meg, beginning to lecture in her elder-sisterly fashion. "You are old enough to leave off boyish tricks, and to behave better, Josephine. It didn't matter so much when you were a little girl, but now you are so tall, and turn up your hair, you should remember that you are a young lady."

"I'm not! And if turning up my hair makes me one, I'll wear it in two tails till I'm twenty," cried Jo, pulling off her net, and shaking down a chestnut mane. "I hate to think I've got to grow up, and be Miss March, and wear long gowns, and look as prim as a China Aster! It's bad enough to be a girl, anyway, when I like boy's games and work and manners! I can't get over my disappointment in not being a boy. And it's worse than ever now, for I'm dying to go and fight with Papa. And I can only stay home and knit, like a poky old woman!"

And Jo shook the blue army sock till the needles rattled like castanets, and her ball bounded across the room.

10. Why does Beth compare her sisters to birds in a nest?   (RL.7.4)

Ⓐ Because they are "pecking" at each other, but not really hurting one another.
Ⓑ Because they all need to learn to "fly" on their own and give their parents some relief.
Ⓒ Because they are gifted musically and should sing together.
Ⓓ Because they are always hungry and calling for someone to feed them.

11. From the passage above, what does the author want the reader to know about Jo?   (RL.7.4)

Ⓐ That she enjoys buying and reading books
Ⓑ That she is selfish
Ⓒ That she knows exactly what she wants and how to get it.
Ⓓ That she is smarter than the other sisters

Excerpt from *War of the Worlds*
H.G. Wells

The Martians seem to have calculated their descent with amazing subtlety—their mathematical learning is evidently far in excess of ours—and to have carried out their preparations with a well-nigh perfect unanimity. Had our instruments permitted it, we might have seen the gathering trouble far back in the nineteenth century. Men like Schiaparelli watched the red planet—it is odd, by the way, that for countless centuries Mars has been the star of war—but failed to interpret the fluctuating appearances of the markings they mapped so well. All that time the Martians must have been getting ready.

12. In the excerpt above, what is the author's tone toward the Martians?   (RL.7.4)

Ⓐ He is impressed by their intelligence and planning.
Ⓑ He finds them inferior to Earth's scientists.
Ⓒ He is afraid of what they will do.
Ⓓ He looks forward to learning from them.

13. In the excerpt above, what is the author's tone toward the scientists of Earth? (RL.7.4)

Ⓐ He forgives them for not seeing the building threat. Their instruments were too primitive. (forgiveness)
Ⓑ He blames them for not developing instruments to identify the building threat on Mars. (anger)
Ⓒ He believes they identified Mars as a source of war early on but didn't share what they knew. (distrustful)
Ⓓ He believes they could have been able to interpret the changes to the surface of the planet and determined what the Martians were planning. (annoyed)

"Dreams"
By Langston Hughes

Hold fast to dreams
For if dreams die
Life is a broken-winged bird
That cannot fly.
Hold fast to dreams
For when dreams go
Life is a barren field
Frozen with snow.

14. What point is the poet making with the comparison in the first stanza?   (RL.7.4)

Ⓐ Without dreams, people cannot make progress in their lives.
Ⓑ Life without dreams is cold and barren.
Ⓒ Like a bird with a broken wing, life is fragile and must be protected.
Ⓓ Even if one cannot fly, he or she can still have a rewarding life.

"Do Not Go Gentle into that Good Night"
Dylan Thomas

Do not go gentle into that good night,
Old age should burn and rave at close of day;
Rage, rage against the dying of the light.
Though wise men at their end know dark is right,
Because their words had forked no lightning they
Do not go gentle into that good night.
Good men, the last wave by, crying how bright
Their frail deeds might have danced in a green bay,
Rage, rage against the dying of the light.
Wild men who caught and sang the sun in flight,
And learn, too late, they grieved it on its way,
Do not go gentle into that good night.
Grave men, near death, who see with blinding sight
Blind eyes could blaze like meteors and be gay,
Rage, rage against the dying of the light.
And you, my father, there on the sad height,
Curse, bless me now with your fierce tears, I pray.
Do not go gentle into that good night.
Rage, rage against the dying of the light.

120

15. Which characteristic of this poem indicates it is a villanelle?   (RL.7.5)

Ⓐ There are two rhyming patterns.
Ⓑ The poem is written in iambic meter.
Ⓒ The subject of the poem is death.
Ⓓ There is a chorus or refrain between every two stanzas.

16. Which answer does not use repetition to develop the tone of this poem?   (RL.7.5)

Ⓐ The word rage is repeated to develop the idea that one can fight back against death.
Ⓑ The word men is repeated to remind the subject about whom he is writing.
Ⓒ The word gentle is repeated to remind the reader how to behave.
Ⓓ The word me is repeated to establish the focus of the poem.

17. How is end rhyme used to make connections between the stanzas?   (RL.7.5)

Ⓐ Every other line rhymes.
Ⓑ Each stanza uses the same rhyme scheme.
Ⓒ The rhyme scheme changes every other stanza.
Ⓓ The last line of each stanza rhymes with the first line of the next stanza.

Ethan Frome
Edith Wharton

I HAD THE STORY, bit by bit, from various people, and, as generally happens in such cases, each time it was a different story.

If you know Starkfield, Massachusetts, you know the post-office. If you know the post-office you must have seen Ethan Frome drive up to it, drop the reins on his hollow-backed bay and drag himself across the brick pavement to the white colonnade; and you must have asked who he was.

It was there that, several years ago, I saw him for the first time; and the sight pulled me up sharp. Even then he was the most striking figure in Starkfield, though he was but the ruin of a man. It was not so much his great height that marked him, for the "natives" were easily singled out by their lank longitude from the stockier foreign breed: it was the careless powerful look he had, in spite of a lameness checking each step like the jerk of a chain. There was something bleak and unapproachable in his face, and he was so stiffened and grizzled that I took him for an old man and was surprised to hear that he was not more than fifty-two. I had this from Harmon Gow, who had driven the stage from Bettsbridge to Starkfield in pre-trolley days and knew the chronicle of all the families on his line.

"He's looked that way ever since he had his smash-up; and that's twenty four years ago come next February," Harmon threw out between reminiscent pauses.

The "smash-up" it was—I gathered from the same informant—which, besides drawing the red gash across Ethan Frome's forehead, had so shortened and warped his right side that it cost him a visible effort to take the few steps from his buggy to the post-office window. He used to drive in from his farm every day at about noon, and as that was my own hour for fetching my mail I often passed him in the porch or stood beside him while we waited on the motions of the distributing hand behind the grating. I noticed that, though he came so punctually, he seldom received anything but a copy of the Bettsbridge Eagle, which he put without a glance into his sagging pocket. At intervals, however, the post-master would hand him an envelope addressed to Mrs. Zenobia —or Mrs. Zeena-Frome, and usually bearing conspicuously in the upper left-hand corner the address of some manufacturer of patent medicine and the name of his specific. These documents my neighbour would also pocket without a glance, as if too much used to them to wonder at their number and variety, and would then turn away with a silent nod to the post-master.

18. What does this prologue to the story, Ethan Frome, suggest about the story that is about to be told?   (RL.7.5)

Ⓐ That it is a true story.
Ⓑ That the story is based in part on rumors heard about town.
Ⓒ That the narrator is not certain of the accuracy of all of the details she is about to present.
Ⓓ That the narrator has known the subject of the story for a long time.

19. Why might the author have included this prologue?   (RL.7.5)

Ⓐ To relieve herself of any responsibility for the story's accuracy.
Ⓑ To explain how she became familiar with the story she is about to tell.
Ⓒ To explain the importance of accuracy in the story that will follow.
Ⓓ To hint at how the story will end.

NOTES

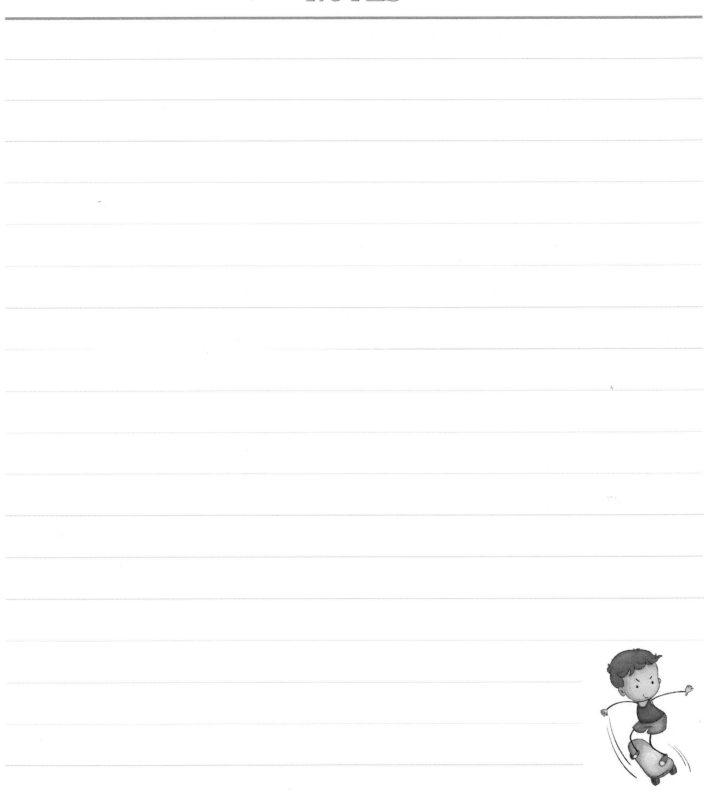

Excerpt from Romeo and Juliet
By William Shakespeare

PROLOGUE

Two households, both alike in dignity,
In fair Verona, where we lay our scene,
From ancient grudge break to new mutiny,
Where civil blood makes civil hands unclean.
From forth the fatal loins of these two foes
A pair of star-cross'd lovers take their life;
Whose misadventured piteous overthrows
Do with their death bury their parents' strife.
The fearful passage of their death-mark'd love,
And the continuance of their parents' rage,
Which, but their children's end, nought could remove,
Is now the two hours' traffic of our stage;
The which if you with patient ears attend,
What here shall miss, our toil shall strive to mend.

SCENE I. Verona. A public place.

Enter SAMPSON and GREGORY, of the house of Capulet, armed with swords and bucklers

SAMPSON
Gregory, o' my word, we'll not carry coals.
GREGORY
No, for then we should be colliers.
SAMPSON
I mean, an we be in choler, we'll draw.
GREGORY
Ay, while you live, draw your neck out o' the collar.
SAMPSON
I strike quickly, being moved.
GREGORY
But thou art not quickly moved to strike.
SAMPSON
A dog of the house of Montague moves me.
GREGORY
To move is to stir; and to be valiant is to stand:
therefore, if thou art moved, thou runn'st away.

SAMPSON
A dog of that house shall move me to stand: I will
take the wall of any man or maid of Montague's.
GREGORY
That shows thee a weak slave; for the weakest goes
to the wall.
SAMPSON
True; and therefore women, being the weaker vessels,
are ever thrust to the wall: therefore I will push
Montague's men from the wall, and thrust his maids
to the wall.
GREGORY
The quarrel is between our masters and us their men.
SAMPSON
'Tis all one, I will show myself a tyrant: when I
have fought with the men, I will be cruel with the
maids, and cut off their heads.
GREGORY
The heads of the maids?
SAMPSON
Ay, the heads of the maids, or their maidenheads;
take it in what sense thou wilt.
GREGORY
They must take it in sense that feel it.
SAMPSON
Me they shall feel while I am able to stand: and
'tis known I am a pretty piece of flesh.
GREGORY
'Tis well thou art not fish; if thou hadst, thou
hadst been poor John. Draw thy tool! here comes
two of the house of the Montagues.
SAMPSON
My naked weapon is out: quarrel, I will back thee.
GREGORY
How! turn thy back and run?
SAMPSON
Fear me not.
GREGORY
No, marry; I fear thee!
SAMPSON
Let us take the law of our sides; let them begin.

GREGORY
I will frown as I pass by, and let them take it as
they list.
SAMPSON
Nay, as they dare. I will bite my thumb at them;
which is a disgrace to them, if they bear it.
Enter ABRAHAM and BALTHASAR

20. What is the difference between the format of the prologue and the rest of this excerpt?

(RL.7.5)

Ⓐ The prologue is written in verse, the rest in prose.
Ⓑ The prologue is written in prose, the rest in verse.
Ⓒ The prologue uses iambic tetrameter and the rest of the excerpt uses iambic pentameter.
Ⓓ There is a difference in the spacing of the lines for easier reading.

"Stopping by Woods on a Snowy Evening"
By Robert Frost

Whose woods these are I think I know.
His house is in the village though;
He will not see me stopping here
To watch his woods fill up with snow.

My little horse must think it queer
To stop without a farmhouse near
Between the woods and frozen lake
The darkest evening of the year.

He gives his harness bells a shake
To ask if there is some mistake.
The only other sound's the sweep
Of easy wind and downy flake.

The woods are lovely, dark and deep.
But I have promises to keep,
And miles to go before I sleep,
And miles to go before I sleep.

Robert Frost, "Stopping by Woods on a Snowy Evening" from The Poetry of Robert Frost, edited by Edward Connery Lathem. Copyright 1923, © 1969 by Henry Holt and Company, Inc., renewed 1951, by Robert Frost. Reprinted with the permission of Henry Holt and Company, LLC.

Source: The Random House Book of Poetry for Children (1983). Retrieved 13, July, 2013.http://www.poetryfoundation.org/poem/171621.

21. What is the rhyme scheme of the first two stanzas?   (RL.7.5)

Ⓐ aabb
    aabb

Ⓑ aabb
    bbaa

Ⓒ abcd
    abcd

Ⓓ aaba
    bbcb

22. What is the effect of this use of personification?   (RL.7.5)

   **"...He gives his harness bells a shake
   As if to ask if there is some mistake..."**

Ⓐ The author likes to use horses in his poetry to show the time in history that the poem was written.
Ⓑ To show the reader that the horse and the man are very close.
Ⓒ The horse's communication emphasises how odd it would be to stop in the woods at that time.
Ⓓ The horse shakes because he is cold and wants the man to hurry.

23. What is the rhyme scheme of this poem?   (RL.7.5)

Ⓐ abaa
    abba
    aaba
    cccc

Ⓑ abaa
    bbcb
    ccdc
    dddd

Ⓒ abcd
    abcd
    abcd
    abcd

Ⓓ abaad
    abaab
    abcdeb
    abdec

"The Road Not Taken"
BY ROBERT FROST

Two roads diverged in a yellow wood,
And sorry I could not travel both
And be one traveler, long I stood
And looked down one as far as I could
To where it bent in the undergrowth;

Then took the other, as just as fair,
And having perhaps the better claim,
Because it was grassy and wanted wear;
Though as for that the passing there
Had worn them really about the same,

And both that morning equally lay
In leaves no step had trodden black.
Oh, I kept the first for another day!
Yet knowing how way leads on to way,
I doubted if I should ever come back.

I shall be telling this with a sigh
Somewhere ages and ages hence:
Two roads diverged in a wood, and I—
I took the one less traveled by,
And that has made all the difference.

24. What line in the last stanza indicates a time in the future?   (RL.7.5)

Ⓐ no step had trodden black
Ⓑ two roads diverged
Ⓒ yellow wood
Ⓓ somewhere ages and ages hence

THE EMPEROR'S NEW CLOTHES
by: Hans Christian Anderson

Many years ago there was an Emperor, who was so excessively fond of new clothes that he spent all his money on them. He cared nothing about his soldiers, nor for the theatre, nor for driving in the woods except for the sake of showing off his new clothes. He had a costume for every hour in the day, and instead of saying, as one does about any other king or emperor, 'He is in his council chamber,' here one always said, 'The Emperor is in his dressing-room.'

Life was very gay in the great town where he lived; hosts of strangers came to visit it every day, and among them one day two swindlers. They gave themselves out as weavers, and said that they knew how to weave the most beautiful stuffs imaginable. Not only were the colours and patterns unusually fine, but the clothes that were made of the stuffs had the peculiar quality of becoming invisible to every person who was not fit for the office he held, or if he was impossibly dull.

Those must be splendid clothes,' thought the Emperor. 'By wearing them I should be able to discover which men in my kingdom are unfitted for their posts. I shall distinguish the wise men from the fools. Yes, I certainly must order some of that stuff to be woven for me.

He paid the two swindlers a lot of money in advance so that they might begin their work at once.

129

They did put up two looms and pretended to weave, but they had nothing whatever upon their shuttles. At the outset they asked for a quantity of the finest silk and the purest gold thread, all of which they put into their own bags, while they worked away at the empty looms far into the night.

I should like to know how those weavers are getting on with the stuff,' thought the Emperor; but he felt a little queer when he reflected that anyone who was stupid or unfit for his post would not be able to see it. He certainly thought that he need have no fears for himself, but still he thought he would send somebody else first to see how it was getting on. Everybody in the town knew what wonderful power the stuff possessed, and everyone was anxious to see how stupid his neighbour was.

I will send my faithful old minister to the weavers,' thought the Emperor. 'He will be best able to see how the stuff looks, for he is a clever man, and no one fulfils his duties better than he does!'

So the good old minister went into the room where the two swindlers sat working at the empty loom.

Heaven preserve us!' thought the old minister, opening his eyes very wide. 'Why, I can't see a thing!' But he took care not to say so.

Both the swindlers begged him to be good enough to step a little nearer, and asked if he did not think it a good pattern and beautiful colouring. They pointed to the empty loom, and the poor old minister stared as hard as he could, but he could not see anything, for of course there was nothing to see.

Good heavens!' thought he, 'is it possible that I am a fool. I have never thought so, and nobody must know it. Am I not fit for my post? It will never do to say that I cannot see the stuffs.

Well, sir, you don't say anything about the stuff,' said the one who was pretending to weave.

Oh, it is beautiful! quite charming!' said the old minister, looking through his spectacles; 'this pattern and these colours! I will certainly tell the Emperor that the stuff pleases me very much.

We are delighted to hear you say so,' said the swindlers, and then they named all the colours and described the peculiar pattern. The old minister paid great attention to what they said, so as to be able to repeat it when he got home to the Emperor.

Then the swindlers went on to demand more money, more silk, and more gold, to be able to proceed with the weaving; but they put it all into their own pockets—not a single strand was ever put into the loom, but they went on as before weaving at the empty loom.

The Emperor soon sent another faithful official to see how the stuff was getting on, and if it would soon be ready. The same thing happened to him as to the minister; he looked and looked, but as there was only the empty loom, he could see nothing at all.

130

Is not this a beautiful piece of stuff?' said both the swindlers, showing and explaining the beautiful pattern and colours which were not there to be seen.

I know I am not a fool!' thought the man, 'so it must be that I am unfit for my good post! It is very strange, though! However, one must not let it appear!' So he praised the stuff he did not see, and assured them of his delight in the beautiful colours and the originality of the design. 'It is absolutely charming!' he said to the Emperor. Everybody in the town was talking about this splendid stuff.

Now the Emperor thought he would like to see it while it was still on the loom. So, accompanied by a number of selected courtiers, among whom were the two faithful officials who had already seen the imaginary stuff, he went to visit the crafty impostors, who were working away as hard as ever they could at the empty loom.

It is magnificent!' said both the honest officials. 'Only see, your Majesty, what a design! What colours!' And they pointed to the empty loom, for they thought no doubt the others could see the stuff.

What!' thought the Emperor; 'I see nothing at all! This is terrible! Am I a fool? Am I not fit to be Emperor? Why, nothing worse could happen to me!
Oh, it is beautiful!' said the Emperor. 'It has my highest approval!' and he nodded his satisfaction as he gazed at the empty loom. Nothing would induce him to say that he could not see anything.

The whole suite gazed and gazed, but saw nothing more than all the others. However, they all exclaimed with his Majesty, 'It is very beautiful!' and they advised him to wear a suit made of this wonderful cloth on the occasion of a great procession which was just about to take place. 'It is magnificent! gorgeous! excellent!' went from mouth to mouth; they were all equally delighted with it.

The Emperor gave each of the rogues an order of knighthood to be worn in their buttonholes and the title of 'Gentlemen weavers.'

The swindlers sat up the whole night, before the day on which the procession was to take place, burning sixteen candles; so that people might see how anxious they were to get the Emperor's new clothes ready. They pretended to take the stuff off the loom. They cut it out in the air with a huge pair of scissors, and they stitched away with needles without any thread in them. At last they said: 'Now the Emperor's new clothes are ready!

The Emperor, with his grandest courtiers, went to them himself, and both the swindlers raised one arm in the air, as if they were holding something, and said: 'See, these are the trousers, this is the coat, here is the mantle!' and so on. 'It is as light as a spider's web. One might think one had nothing on, but that is the very beauty of it!'

Yes!' said all the courtiers, but they could not see anything, for there was nothing to see.

Will your imperial majesty be graciously pleased to take off your clothes,' said, the impostors, 'so that we may put on the new ones, along here before the great mirror?'

The Emperor took off all his clothes, and the impostors pretended to give him one article of dress after the other of the new ones which they had pretended to make. They pretended to fasten something round his waist and to tie on something; this was the train, and the Emperor turned round and round in front of the mirror.

How well his majesty looks in the new clothes! How becoming they are!' cried all the people round. 'What a design, and what colours! They are most gorgeous robes!'
The canopy is waiting outside which is to be carried over your majesty in the procession,' said the master of the ceremonies.

Well, I am quite ready,' said the Emperor. 'Don't the clothes fit well?' and then he turned round again in front of the mirror, so that he should seem to be looking at his grand things.

The chamberlains who were to carry the train stooped and pretended to lift it from the ground with both hands, and they walked along with their hands in the air. They dared not let it appear that they could not see anything.

Then the Emperor walked along in the procession under the gorgeous canopy, and everybody in the streets and at the windows exclaimed, 'How beautiful the Emperor's new clothes are! What a splendid train! And they fit to perfection!' Nobody would let it appear that he could see nothing, for then he would not be fit for his post, or else he was a fool.

None of the Emperor's clothes had been so successful before.

But he has got nothing on,' said a little child.

Oh, listen to the innocent,' said its father; and one person whispered to the other what the child had said. 'He has nothing on; a child says he has nothing on!

But he has nothing on!' at last cried all the people.

The Emperor writhed, for he knew it was true, but he thought 'the procession must go on now,' so held himself stiffer than ever, and the chamberlains held up the invisible train.

25. Which excerpt from the text provides the reason the Emperor agreed to buy clothes from the swindlers?   (RL.7.6)

Ⓐ Not only were the colors and patterns unusually fine, but the clothes that were made of the stuffs had the peculiar quality of becoming invisible to every person who was not fit for the office he held, or if he was impossibly dull.

Ⓑ Life was very gay in the great town where he lived; hosts of strangers came to visit it every day, and among them one day two swindlers. They gave themselves out as weavers, and said that they knew how to weave the most beautiful stuffs imaginable.

Ⓒ At the outset they asked for a quantity of the finest silk and the purest gold thread, all of which they put into their own bags, while they worked away at the empty looms far into the night.

Ⓓ 'I know I am not a fool!' thought the man, 'so it must be that I am unfit for my good post! It is very strange, though! However, one must not let it appear!' So he praised the stuff he did not see, and assured them of his delight in the beautiful colours and the originality of the design.

26. What character trait do the Emperor and his minister share?   (RL.7.6)

Ⓐ They are both insecure about their qualifications.
Ⓑ They both want to fool the public
Ⓒ They both want the Emperor to have the most wonderful clothing available.
Ⓓ Both men are able to imagine things that are not visible.

27. Why does the Emperor continue with the procession after the child reviews the truth?   (RL.7.6)

Ⓐ He doesn't believe the child.
Ⓑ He doesn't want to admit to his subjects that the swindlers had tricked him.
Ⓒ He is concerned that there are people in the audience who can see the clothes.
Ⓓ He has paid for his new clothes and wants to continue showing them off.

NOTES

Huckleberry Finn (Excerpt)
By Mark Twain

In this excerpt from Chapter Five, Huck's father arrives unexpectedly.

I HAD shut the door to. Then I turned around and there he was. I used to be scared of him all the time, he beat me so much. I reckoned I was scared now, too; but in a minute I see I was mistaken -- that is, after the first jolt, as you may say, when my breath sort of hitched, he being so unexpected; but right away after I see I warn't scared of him worth bothring about.

He was most fifty, and he looked it. His hair was long and tangled and greasy, and hung down, and you could see his eyes shining through like he was behind vines. It was all black, no gray; so was his long, mixed-up whiskers. There warn't no color in his face, where his face showed; it was white; not like another man's white, but a white to make a body sick, a white to make a body's flesh crawl -- a tree-toad white, a fish-belly white. As for his clothes -- just rags, that was all. He had one ankle resting on t'other knee; the boot on that foot was busted, and two of his toes stuck through, and he worked them now and then. His hat was laying on the floor -- an old black slouch with the top caved in, like a lid.

I stood a-looking at him; he set there a-looking at me, with his chair tilted back a little. I set the candle down. I noticed the window was up; so he had climbed in by the shed. He kept a-looking me all over. By and by he says:
"Starchy clothes -- very. You think you're a good deal of a big-bug, don't you?"

"Maybe I am, maybe I ain't," I says.

"Don't you give me none o' your lip," says he. "You've put on considerable many frills since I been away. I'll take you down a peg before I get done with you. You're educated, too, they say -- can read and write. You think you're better'n your father, now, don't you, because he can't? I'll take it out of you. Who told you you might meddle with such hifalut'n foolishness, hey? -- who told you you could?"

"The widow. She told me."

"The widow, hey? -- and who told the widow she could put in her shovel about a thing that ain't none of her business?"

"Nobody never told her."

"Well, I'll learn her how to meddle. And looky here -- you drop that school, you hear? I'll learn people to bring up a boy to put on airs over his own father and let on to be better'n what he is. You lemme catch you fooling around that school again, you hear? Your mother couldn't read, and she couldn't write, nuther, before she died. None of the family couldn't before they died. I can't; and here you're a-swelling yourself up like this. I ain't the man to stand it -- you hear? Say, lemme hear you read."

I took up a book and begun something about General Washington and the wars. When I'd read about a half a minute, he fetched the book a whack with his hand and knocked it across the house. He says:
"It's so. You can do it. I had my doubts when you told me. Now looky here; you stop that putting on frills. I won't have it. I'll lay for you, my smarty; and if I catch you about that school I'll tan you good. First you know you'll get religion, too. I never see such a son.

He took up a little blue and yaller picture of some cows and a boy, and says:
"What's this?"
"It's something they give me for learning my lessons good."

He tore it up, and says:
"I'll give you something better -- I'll give you a cowhide.

He set there mumbling for a minute, and then he says:
"*Ain't* you a sweet-scented dandy, though? A bed; and bedclothes; and a look'n'-glass; and a piece of carpet on the floor -- and your own father got to sleep with the hogs in the tanyard. I never see such a son. I bet I'll take some o' these frills out o' you before I'm done with you. Why, there ain't no end to your airs -- they say you're rich. Hey? -- how's that?"

"They lie -- that's how."
"Looky here -- mind how you talk to me; I'm a-standing about all I can stand now -- so don't gimme no sass. I've been in town two days, and I hain't heard nothing but about you bein' rich. I heard about it away down the river, too. That's why I come. You git me that money to-morrow -- I want it."
"I hain't got no money."
"It's a lie. Judge Thatcher's got it. You git it. I want it."
"I hain't got no money, I tell you. You ask Judge Thatcher; he'll tell you the same."
"All right. I'll ask him; and I'll make him pungle, too, or I'll know the reason why. Say, how much you got in your pocket? I want it."
"I hain't got only a dollar, and I want that to -- "
"It don't make no difference what you want it for -- you just shell it out."

28. Why might Huck be afraid of his father?   (RL.7.6)

Ⓐ His father has beaten him in the past.
Ⓑ Huck hasn't been attending school and is afraid his father will be angry.
Ⓒ He is afraid his father will hurt his friends.
Ⓓ His father has threatened to take him away from his friends.

29. What does Huck's father want Huck to do after Huck demonstrates that he knows how to read?   (RL.7.6)

Ⓐ He tells Huck he's proud of him and then asks for Huck's money.

Ⓑ He hits the book out of Huck's hands and flings it across the room, then tells Huck to stop showin off.

Ⓒ He tells Huck to stop attending school.

Ⓓ He asks Huck to teach him how to read.

The Call of the Wild Excerpt by Jack London

Buck lived at a big house in the sun-kissed Santa Clara Valley. Judge Miller's place, it was called. It stood back from the road, half hidden among the trees, through which glimpses could be caught of the wide cool veranda that ran around its four sides. The house was approached by gravelled driveways which wound about through wide-spreading lawns and under the interlacing boughs of tall poplars. At the rear things were on even a more spacious scale than at the front. There were great stables, where a dozen grooms and boys held forth, rows of vine-clad servants' cottages, an endless and orderly array of out-houses, long grape arbors, green pastures, orchards, and berry patches. Then there was the pumping plant for the artesian well, and the big cement tank where Judge Miller's boys took their morning plunge and kept cool in the hot afternoon. And over this great demesne Buck ruled. Here he was born, and here he had lived the four years of his life. It was true, there were other dogs, There could not but be other dogs on so vast a place, but they did not count. They came and went, resided in the populous kennels, or lived obscurely in the recesses of the house after the fashion of Toots, the Japanese pug, or Ysabel, the Mexican hairless,--strange creatures that rarely put nose out of doors or set foot to ground. On the other hand, there were the fox terriers, a score of them at least, who yelped fearful promises at Toots and Ysabel looking out of the windows at them and protected by a legion of housemaids armed with brooms and mops. But Buck was neither house-dog nor kennel-dog. The whole realm was his. He plunged into the swimming tank or went hunting with the Judge's sons; he escorted Mollie and Alice, the Judge's daughters, on long twilight or early morning rambles; on wintry nights he lay at the Judge's feet before the roaring library fire; he carried the Judge's grandsons on his back, or rolled them in the grass, and guarded their footsteps through wild adventures down to the fountain in the stable yard, and even beyond, where the paddocks were, and the berry patches. Among the terriers he stalked imperiously, and Toots and Ysabel he utterly ignored, for he was king,--king over all creeping, crawling, flying things of Judge Miller's place, humans included.

30. Why does Buck "utterly ignore" Toots and Ysabel?   (RL.7.6)

Ⓐ Their names are strange.

Ⓑ The other two dogs don't act the way he feels a dog should behave.

Ⓒ He's not allowed inside, so he thinks it is odd that they are.

Ⓓ The other two dogs tease him.

31. What made Buck proud of being "neither a house-dog or a kennel-dog?"   (RL.7.6)

Ⓐ The judge told him so.
Ⓑ Buck chose that life.
Ⓒ Buck was part of family events.
Ⓓ Buck had been with the Miller's longer than other dogs.

32. The quote "...strange creatures that rarely put nose out of doors or set foot to ground..." tells the reader what about Toots and Ysabel?   (RL.7.6)

Ⓐ Their names are odd, and so are they.
Ⓑ They are too little to be outside.
Ⓒ They are "babied" in the house and behave like people.
Ⓓ There are too many dogs outside already.

33. What is Buck's mood in this excerpt?   (RL.7.6)

Ⓐ weary and wishful
Ⓑ relaxed and relieved
Ⓒ joyful and jaded
Ⓓ desperate and dejected

34. Based on the excerpts from *The Call of the Wild*, all of these can describe Buck EXCEPT_____?   (RL.7.6)

Ⓐ honorable
Ⓑ persistent
Ⓒ grateful
Ⓓ aggressive

"Love Between Brothers and Sister" by Isaac Watts

Whatever brawls disturb the street,

There should be peace at home;

Where sisters dwell and brothers meet,

Quarrels should never come.

Birds in their little nests agree;

And 'tis a shameful sight,

When children of one family

Fall out and chide and fight.

35. Which statement contrasts with the author's viewpoint in this poem?   (RL.7.7)

Ⓐ Brothers and sisters should try their hardest to love one another.
Ⓑ Nothing good can come from siblings arguing with one another.
Ⓒ There's no harm in siblings occasionally not getting along with one another.
Ⓓ It is natural for siblings to have arguments.

TO MAKE AN AMBLONGUS PIE. by Edward Lear

Take 4 pounds (say 4½ pounds) of fresh Amblongusses, and put them in a small pipkin.

Cover them with water, and boil them for 8 hours incessantly; after which add 2 pints of new milk, and proceed to boil for 4 hours more.

When you have ascertained that the Amblongusses are quite soft, take them out, and place them in a wide pan, taking care to shake them well previously.

Grate some nutmeg over the surface, and cover them carefully with powdered gingerbread, curry-powder, and a sufficient quantity of Cayenne pepper.

Remove the pan into the next room, and place it on the floor. Bring it back again, and let it simmer for three-quarters of an hour. Shake the pan violently till all the Amblongusses have become of a pale purple color.

Then, having prepared the paste, insert the whole carefully; adding at the same time a small pigeon, 2 slices of beef, 4 cauliflowers, and any number of oysters.

Watch patiently till the crust begins to rise, and add a pinch of salt from time to time.
Serve up in a clean dish, and throw the whole out of window as fast as possible.

36. How is this recipe different than a typical recipe?   (RL.7.7)

Ⓐ This recipe is nonsense while real recipes are intended to be made.
Ⓑ The directions in this recipe are out of order while real recipes present the directions in the order they are intended to be followed in.
Ⓒ This recipe uses exotic ingredients while typical recipes use common ingredients.
Ⓓ This recipe is much more time consuming than a typical recipe.

A VALENTINE TO CATHERINE by Evaleen Stein

If you will be my True-Love,
I'll tell you what I'll do,
I'll ask a little bluebird
To sing a song to you.

When first you see a violet
And softly pricking through
The garden-bed come crocuses
And golden tulips, too,

Then watch! for he'll be coming,
The little bird of blue;
He'll sing, "I love you, Sweetheart,
It's true, true, true!"

37. How is this Valentine poem unlike the valentines people exchange on Valentine's Day today?   (RL.7.7)

Ⓐ The poem and valentines show love for the people they are given to.
Ⓑ The poem and valentines have "I love you" written in them.
Ⓒ The poem and valentines have birds in them.
Ⓓ There is no difference in either types of cards.

From "The Strike of the Fireworks" by Carolyn Wells

'Twas the night before the Fourth of July, the people slept serene;
The fireworks were stored in the old town hall that stood on the village green.
The steeple clock tolled the midnight hour, and at its final stroke,
The fire in the queer old-fashioned stove lifted its voice and spoke;
"The earth and air have naught to do, the water, too, may play,
And only fire is made to work on Independence Day.

38. How is the scene described in this stanza of the poem typical of a Fourth of July celebration?   (RL.7.7)

Ⓐ The people in town go to bed early on the Fourth of July.
Ⓑ There is a fireworks celebration held in the town on the Fourth of July.
Ⓒ There is a bonfire on the Fourth of July.
Ⓓ There is a town clock that strikes midnight.

NOTES

"Paul Revere's Ride" (Excerpt)
Henry Wadsworth Longfellow

Listen my children and you shall hear
Of the midnight ride of Paul Revere,
On the eighteenth of April, in Seventy-five;
Hardly a man is now alive
Who remembers that famous day and year.
He said to his friend, "If the British march
By land or sea from the town to-night,
Hang a lantern aloft in the belfry arch
Of the North Church tower as a signal light,--
One if by land, and two if by sea;
And I on the opposite shore will be,
Ready to ride and spread the alarm
Through every Middlesex village and farm,
For the country folk to be up and to arm."
Then he said "Good-night!" and with muffled oar
Silently rowed to the Charlestown shore,
Just as the moon rose over the bay,
Where swinging wide at her moorings lay
The Somerset, British man-of-war;
A phantom ship, with each mast and spar
Across the moon like a prison bar,
And a huge black hulk, that was magnified
By its own reflection in the tide.

It was twelve by the village clock
When he crossed the bridge into Medford town.
He heard the crowing of the cock,
And the barking of the farmer's dog,
And felt the damp of the river fog,
That rises after the sun goes down.
It was one by the village clock,
When he galloped into Lexington.
He saw the gilded weathercock
Swim in the moonlight as he passed,
And the meeting-house windows, black and bare,
Gaze at him with a spectral glare,
As if they already stood aghast
At the bloody work they would look upon.

It was two by the village clock,
When he came to the bridge in Concord town.

He heard the bleating of the flock,
And the twitter of birds among the trees,
And felt the breath of the morning breeze
Blowing over the meadow brown.
And one was safe and asleep in his bed
Who at the bridge would be first to fall,
Who that day would be lying dead,
Pierced by a British musket ball.
You know the rest. In the books you have read
How the British Regulars fired and fled,---
How the farmers gave them ball for ball,
From behind each fence and farmyard wall,
Chasing the redcoats down the lane,
Then crossing the fields to emerge again
Under the trees at the turn of the road,
And only pausing to fire and load.

The Real Story of Revere's Ride
From the Paul Revere House official Website
In 1774 and the Spring of 1775 Paul Revere was employed by the Boston Committee of Correspondence and the Massachusetts Committee of Safety as an express rider to carry news, messages, and copies of resolutions as far away as New York and Philadelphia.

On the evening of April 18, 1775, Paul Revere was sent for by Dr. Joseph Warren and instructed to ride to Lexington, Massachusetts, to warn Samuel Adams and John Hancock that British troops were marching to arrest them. After being rowed across the Charles River to Charlestown by two associates, Paul Revere borrowed a horse from his friend Deacon John Larkin. While in Charlestown, he verified that the local "Sons of Liberty" committee had seen his pre-arranged signals. (Two lanterns had been hung briefly in the bell-tower of Christ Church in Boston, indicating that troops would row "by sea" across the Charles River to Cambridge, rather than marching "by land" out Boston Neck. Revere had arranged for these signals the previous weekend, as he was afraid that he might be prevented from leaving Boston).

On the way to Lexington, Revere "alarmed" the country-side, stopping at each house, and arrived in Lexington about midnight. As he approached the house where Adams and Hancock were staying, a sentry asked that he not make so much noise. "Noise!" cried Revere, "You'll have noise enough before long. The regulars are coming out!" After delivering his message, Revere was joined by a second rider, William Dawes, who had been sent on the same errand by a different route. Deciding on their own to continue on to Concord, Massachusetts, where weapons and supplies were hidden, Revere and Dawes were joined by a third rider, Dr. Samuel Prescott. Soon after, all three were arrested by a British patrol. Prescott escaped almost immediately, and Dawes soon after. Revere was held for some time and then released. Left without a horse, Revere returned to Lexington in time to witness part of the battle on the Lexington Green.

39. According to the poem, what was the purpose of Revere's ride?   (RL.7.9)

Ⓐ To alert everyone in the county that the British were approaching.
Ⓑ To warn Samuel Adams and John Hancock that the British were approaching.
Ⓒ To make it back to Boston in time for the battle.
Ⓓ To reach Lexington before the British troops to awaken the members of the militia.

40. According to the non-fiction passage, what was the purpose of Revere's ride? (RL.7.9)

Ⓐ To alert everyone in the county that the British were approaching.
Ⓑ To warn Samuel Adams and John Hancock that the British were approaching.
Ⓒ To make it back to Boston in time for the battle.
Ⓓ To reach Lexington before the British troops to awaken the members of the militia.

41. What information from the non-fiction passage does the poem exclude?   (RL.7.9)

Ⓐ The description of the signals in the church steeple.
Ⓑ That Revere was arrested and held by the British.
Ⓒ That Revere reached the town of Lexington.
Ⓓ That the British soldiers were coming by sea.

42. Which excerpt from the non-fiction passage conflicts most with the poem?   (RL.7.9)

Ⓐ Left without a horse, Revere returned to Lexington in time to witness part of the battle on the Lexington Green.
Ⓑ Paul Revere borrowed a horse from his friend, Deacon John Larkin.
Ⓒ Two lanterns had been hung briefly in the bell-tower of Christ Church in Boston, indicating that troops would row "by sea" across the Charles River to Cambridge, rather than marching "by land" out Boston Neck.
Ⓓ On the way to Lexington, Revere "alarmed" the country-side, stopping at each house, and arrived in Lexington about midnight.

43. About whom might Longfellow have just as accurately written this poem? (RL.7.9)

Ⓐ Samuel Adams
Ⓑ John Larkin
Ⓒ Samuel Prescott
Ⓓ William Dawes

THE BAND OF THE TITANIC
By Florence Earle Coates
"These are the immortal,—the fearless"—*Upanishads*

UP, lads! they say we've struck a berg, though there's no danger yet,—
Our noble liner was not built to wreck!—
But women may have felt a shock they're needing to forget,
And when there's trouble, men should be on deck.

Come!—now's the time! They're wanting us to brighten them a bit;
Play up, my lads—as lively as you can!
Give them a merry English air! they want no counterfeit
Like that down-hearted tune you just began!...

I think the Captain's worried, lads: maybe the thing's gone wrong;
Well, we will show them all is right with us!
Of Drake and the Armadas now we'll play them such a song
Shall make them of the hero emulous.

When boats are being lowered, lads, your place and mine are here,—
Oh, we were never needed more than now!
When others go, it is for us those left behind to cheer,
And I am glad, my lads, that we know how!

If it is Death that's calling us, we'll make a brave response;
Play up, play up!—ye may not play again;
The prize that Nelson won at last, the chance that comes but once,
Is ours, my lads!—the chance to die like men!

From The Worcester Evening Gazette
April 20, 1912

New York, April 19.-Of all the heroes who went to their death when the Titanic dived to its ocean grave, none, in the opinion of Miss Hilda Slater, a passenger in the last boat to pull off, deserved greater credit than the members of the vessel's orchestra. According to Miss Slater, the orchestra played until the last. When the vessel took its final plunge the strains of a lively air, mingled gruesomely with the cries of those who realized that they were face to face with death.

"It was terrible," said Miss Slater, who had come from her home in England to visit a brother, an architect in this city. "From the moment the vessel struck, or as soon as the members of the orchestra could be collected, there was a steady round of lively airs. It did much to keep up the spirits of every-one and probably served as much as the efforts of the officers trying to prevent panic."

When the ship struck the iceberg, Miss Slater went on deck. She was ordered to go back to bed, which she did on being assured there was no danger. A half-hour later she heard confusion on deck and heard someone cry, "Order everyone to don life belts."

After dressing again, Miss. Slater returned to the deck and was ordered to the boat deck aloft.

"When I got there," she said, "I found an indescribable scene. A number of the steerage men pas-sengers had attempted to seize one of the boats and there was a brisk revolver fire: many men fell under it. The prompt, and drastic action of the officers restored order."

"There were many touching scenes as the boats put off. I saw Col. John Jacob Astor hand his young wife into a boat tenderly and then asked an officer whether he might also go. When permission was refused he stepped back and coolly took out his cigarette case. "Good-bye, dearie" he called gaily, as he lighted a cigarette and leaned over the rail. "I'll join you later." Another man, a Frenchman, I think, approached one of the boats about to be lowered. He had with him two little boys. An officer waved him back sternly. "Bless you'" he said "I don't want to go, but for God's sake take the boys. Their mother is waiting for them in New York." The boys were taken aboard."

From The Worcester Evening Gazette
April 20, 1912

New York, April 19- Mrs. John Murray Brown of Acton, Mass, who with her sister, Mrs. Robert C. Cornell and Mrs. E.D. Appleton, was saved, was in the last life-boat to get safely away from the Titanic.

"The band played marching from deck to deck, and as the ship went under I could still hear the mu-sic." Mrs. Brown said. "The musicians were up to their knees in water when last I saw them. We offered assistance to Capt. Smith, but he refused."

"Mrs. Astor was in the life-boat with my sister, Mrs. Cornell. I heard Col. Astor tell her he would wait with the men. Our boat was almost dragged down by the suction."

44. Based on the two newspaper articles, what information from the poem can be confirmed as fact? (RL.7.9)

Ⓐ The band played because they were cold.
Ⓑ The musicians had no intentions of trying to save themselves.
Ⓒ The musicians played so that women would forget the horror of the sinking.
Ⓓ The band played as people were loaded into the lifeboats.

45. What detail from the newspaper articles supports the attitude assigned to the musicians in the last stanza of the poem? (RL.7.9)

Ⓐ "The band played marching from deck to deck, and as the ship went under I could still hear the music. Mrs. Brown said."
Ⓑ "The musicians were up to their knees in water when last I saw them."
Ⓒ "From the moment the vessel struck, or as soon as the members of the orchestra could be collected, there was a steady round of lively airs. It did much to keep up the spirits of everyone and probably served as much as the efforts of the officers trying to prevent panic."
Ⓓ "Another man, a Frenchman, I think, approached one of the boats about to be lowered. He had with him two little boys. An officer waved him back sternly."

46. What detail from the newspaper articles supports the information in the second stanza of the poem? (RL.7.9)

Ⓐ When the vessel took its final plunge, the strains of a lively air mingled gruesomely with the cries of those who realized that they were face to face with death.
Ⓑ "The band played marching from deck to deck, and as the ship went under I could still hear the music." Mrs. Brown said.
Ⓒ Of all the heroes who went to their death when the Titanic dived to its ocean grave, none, in the opinion of Miss. Hilda Slater, a passenger in the last boat to pull off, deserved greater credit than the embers of the vessel's orchestra.
Ⓓ When the ship struck the iceberg, Miss Slater went on deck. She was ordered to go back to bed, which she did on being assured there was no danger.

47. What do both the poem and newspaper articles suggest the ship's band did for the victims and survivors? (RL.7.9)

Ⓐ Provided entertainment while the passengers awaited rescue
Ⓑ Helped organize the lifeboats so that only women and children had places
Ⓒ Helped people from becoming hysterical while the lifeboats were lowered
Ⓓ Helped lower the lifeboats into the water

48. Why would readers consider Mrs. Brown and Miss Slater accurate reporters of what was happening on board the Titanic just before the ship sank? (RL.7.9)

Ⓐ They were personal friends of the members of the band.
Ⓑ They were on the ship until it sank and were rescued from the water.
Ⓒ They were on lifeboats as the ship was sinking.
Ⓓ Their stories offer identical details.

Scientists in South Korea have developed a type of artificial skin that will allow robots to feel slight vibrations. This skin, developed by weaving together extremely small nanohairs made of polymer or plastic is more sensitive than human skin. When vibration is applied to this artificial skin, the nano-hairs bend against each other to generate an electrical current. Sensors within the skin evaluate the current and using that information determine the source of the vibration.
Researchers are excited about the potential for this new development. The artificial skin could be used to cover prosthetic limbs to help those who have lost a limb experience more realistic sensations and function more naturally.
http://en.wikipedia.org/wiki/Neuroplasticity

49. Which sentence best explains why scientists are developing the artificial skin? (RI.7.1)

Ⓐ "The artificial skin could be used to cover prosthetic limbs to help lose who have lost a limb experience more realistic sensations and function more naturally."
Ⓑ "Sensors within the skin evaluate the current and using that information determine the source of the vibration."
Ⓒ "This skin, developed by weaving together extremely small nanohairs made of polymer or plastic is more sensitive than human skin."
Ⓓ "Scientists in South Korea have developed a type of skin that will allow robots to feel slight vibrations."

Diabetic Help

Researchers at pharmaceutical company Eli Lilly and an association that places assistance dogs in Indianapolis, IN are working together on an exciting new project that will study how dogs are able to detect low blood sugar in their diabetic owners. Diabetics suffer from a condition by which the pancreas does not produce enough insulin to maintain a healthy level of blood glucose. If a diabetic person's blood glucose level drops too low, he or she may become unconscious or even go into a coma.

One dog who has had a lot of success in identifying low blood sugar is a two year old named Pete. Pete, like all dogs, has a sense of smell 10,000 times more sensitive than that of humans. Pete's owner is a scientist with Eli Lilly and she is trying to figure out what is inside a dog's nose that makes it possible to smell low blood sugar. If the researcher can figure out how to reproduce that kind of sensitivity, more diabetic people can be protected from the consequences of low blood sugar.

Until the researchers isolate what is inside Pete's nose, the Indiana Canine Assistance Network will continue to train dogs like Pete. It's a slow and expensive process though. In the last ten years, the organization has trained 100 dogs, and the training has cost $25,000 or more for each dog.
http://www.diabetesadvocacy.com/diabetes_news.htm

50. Which sentence from this article best explains how dogs can help diabetic owners?
(RI.7.1)

Ⓐ "In the last ten years, the organization has trained 100 dogs, and the training has cost $25,000 or more for each dog."

Ⓑ "If the researcher can figure out how to reproduce that kind of sensitivity, more diabetic people can be protected from the consequences of low blood sugar."

Ⓒ "Pete's owner is a scientist with Eli Lilly and she is trying to figure out what is inside a dog's nose that makes it possible to smell low blood sugar."

Ⓓ "If a diabetic person's glucose drops too low he or she may become unconscious or even drop into a coma."

51. Based on the sentence, "if the researcher can figure out how to reproduce that sensitivity, more diabetic people can be protected from the consequences of low blood sugar," you can infer that...
(RI.7.1)

Ⓐ The researcher wants to come up with technology that can help detect low blood sugar similar to how dogs can detect low blood sugar.

Ⓑ The researcher wants to breed more dogs with the same sensitivity to low blood sugar as Pete.

Ⓒ The researcher wants to train more dogs to detect low blood sugar levels in diabetic patients.

Ⓓ The researcher wants to reproduce the same sensitivity in herself so she can detect low blood sugar levels in diabetic patients.

52. Which sentence from the passage best explains why scientists want to reproduce the sensitivity rather than simply training dogs to recognize the sensitivity? (RI.7.1)

Ⓐ "It's a slow and expensive process though."

Ⓑ "Until the researchers isolate what is inside Pete's nose, the Indiana Canine Assistance Network will continue to train dogs like Pete."

Ⓒ Pete's owner is a scientist with Eli Lilly and she's trying to figure out what is inside a dog's nose that makes it possible to smell low blood sugar.

Ⓓ "One dog who has had a lot of success in identifying low blood sugar is a two year old named Pete."

Class Rules and Expectations
7th Grade-Reading

1. NO HUNTING! Be nice.
2. No gum allowed.
3. You must be in your seat when the bell rings. If you are not, you are tardy and appropriate consequences will be enforced.
4. Students start the class...not the bell.
5. Make-up work is the student's responsibility.
6. No rude gestures or comments. If you cannot say something nice, do not say anything at all.
7. Have all of your materials with you and ready at the beginning of class.
8. There are no dumb questions...ask if you do not understand.
10. Respect others. This includes teachers as well as students.
11. Keep your hands and feet to yourself.
13. Every student will learn and have fun.

53. Which rule explains what happens if a student is late to class? (RI.7.1)

Ⓐ Rule 3
Ⓑ Rule 4
Ⓒ Rule 5
Ⓓ Rule 8

The Assassination of President Lincoln
April 14, 1865

Shortly after 10 p.m. on April 14, 1865, actor John Wilkes Booth entered the presidential box at Ford's Theatre in Washington D.C., and fatally shot President Abraham Lincoln. As Lincoln slumped forward in his seat, Booth leapt onto the stage and escaped through the back door. A doctor in the audience rushed over to examine the paralyzed president. Lincoln was then carried across the street to Petersen's Boarding House, where he died early the next morning.

Lincoln was the first president assassinated in U.S. history. Why did Booth do it? He thought it would aid the South, which had just surrendered to Federal forces. It had nearly the opposite effect, ending Lincoln's plans for a rather generous peace. Booth did not act alone. This "wanted" poster appeared everywhere, offering a reward for the arrest of Booth and his accomplices. The conspirators were all captured, and Booth was shot while trying to escape from Union soldiers.

The whole country grieved the death of President Lincoln. As the nine-car funeral train carried President Lincoln home for burial in Springfield, Illinois, people showed up at train stations all along the way to pay their respects.

"The Assassination of President Lincoln." The Assassination of President Lincoln. N.p., n.d. Web. 15 July 2013.

http://www.americaslibrary.gov/jb/civil/jb_civil_lincoln_1.html

54. Which sentence best explains why Booth shot Lincoln?   (RI.7.1)

Ⓐ "He thought it would aid the South, which had just surrendered to Federal forces."
Ⓑ "It had nearly the opposite effect, ending Lincoln's plans for a rather generous peace."
Ⓒ "This "wanted" poster appeared everywhere, offering a reward for the arrest of Booth and his accomplices."
Ⓓ "The conspirators were all captured, and Booth was shot while trying to escape from Union soldiers."

55. Which detail in the first sentence helps you infer how Booth was able to get access to the theater?   (RI.7.1)

Ⓐ It was 10 p.m.
Ⓑ He was an actor.
Ⓒ He was going to the presidential box.
Ⓓ It was on April 14.

Gettysburg Address

Four score and seven years ago our fathers brought forth on this continent, a new nation, conceived in liberty, and dedicated to the proposition that all men are created equal.

Now we are engaged in a great civil war, testing whether that nation, or any nation so conceived and so dedicated, can long endure. We are met on a great battlefield of that war. We have come to dedicate a portion of that field, as a final resting place for those who here gave their lives that that nation might live. It is altogether fitting and proper that we should do this.

But in a larger sense, we cannot dedicate - we cannot consecrate - we cannot hallow - this ground. The brave men, living and dead, who struggled here, have consecrated it, far above our poor power to add or detract. The world will little note, nor long remember, what we say here, but it can never forget what they did here. It is for us the living, rather, to be dedicated here to the unfinished work which they who fought here have thus far so nobly advanced. It is rather for us to be here dedicated to the great task remaining before us - that from these honored dead we take increased devotion to that cause for which they gave the last full measure of devotion - that we here highly resolve that these dead shall not have died in vain - that this nation, under God, shall have a new birth of freedom - and that government of the people, by the people, for the people, shall not perish from the earth.

President Abraham Lincoln - November 19, 1863

56. What is Lincoln's purpose in delivering this speech?   (RI.7.2)

Ⓐ To encourage people to not give up on the country being united as one country
Ⓑ To encourage people to end the war and honor the dead
Ⓒ To convince the south to surrender so that it would end more quickly
Ⓓ To build a new cemetery at this location

The bread-and-butter of the film industry is the action movie. Each summer, audiences can expect to see car chases, gunfights and explosions, and studios can expect to see millions and millions of dollars in return. Though most viewers and critics see these movies as "fluff" entertainment, there is one director who puts as much heart and soul into his "fluff" as any number of talented directors put into their "serious" movies. His name is John Woo. Even though you may not have heard about him, he is widely considered to be the best contemporary director of action films working anywhere.

John Woo, after many years of hard work, has become known as the world's best action film director. His action sequences have become the stuff of legend and are now the basis from which all other action movies are judged. More importantly, along with the bloodshed, Woo has proven that he can create real characters with real emotions that the audience can sympathize with.

He's a bold visual stylist who stages kinetic scene of over-the-top gunplay with fluid camera movements, extremely long takes, and perfectly timed choreography of movement. Woo's on the spot improvising that also delivered one of the most amazing gun blazing sequences when in the middle of the movie a full-blooded gunfight erupts, but is played out in balletic slow-motion to "Somewhere Over The Rainbow", heard through child's headphones. The song was put in to the represent the child's innocence, and also to show how that innocence is being corrupted by the violence around him. Woo gets upset when he hears about violence, and when he is angry and directing he thinks, "lets hit the villain with more bullets, lets beat him up just a little bit more."

Woo considers himself to be an artist, as he does once in a while get emotional while filming one of his movies. This goes to show that he relates his movies well to real life, and has an understanding of what it takes to become a great director.

http://www.hollywoodauditions.com/news/celebrities/directors.htm

57. What is an appropriate title for this article?   (RI.7.2)

Ⓐ John Woo Puts the Action in Action!
Ⓑ A History of Action Movies
Ⓒ The Director who Hates Violence
Ⓓ Somewhere over the Rainbow

NOTES

Read the following <u>Aesop's Fable</u> and answer the question below.

In a field one summer's day a Grasshopper was hopping about, chirping and singing to its heart's content. An Ant passed by, bearing along with great toil an ear of corn he was taking to the nest.

"Why not come and chat with me," said the Grasshopper, "instead of toiling and moiling in that way?"
"I am helping to lay up food for the winter," said the Ant, "and recommend you to do the same."
"Why bother about winter?" said the Grasshopper; we have got plenty of food at present." But the Ant went on its way and continued its toil.

When the winter came the Grasshopper found itself dying of hunger, while it saw the ants distributing, every day, corn and grain from the stores they had collected in the summer.

Then the Grasshopper knew...
It is best to prepare for the days of necessity.

58. What type of relationship do the Grasshopper and the Ant have?   (RI.7.3)

Ⓐ The Ant and the Grasshopper might be best friends and always help each other.
Ⓑ The Ant and the Grasshopper might be enemies and never help each other.
Ⓒ The Ant and the Grasshopper might be acquaintances and have different ways of life.
Ⓓ The Ant and the Grasshopper are related to each other.

59. What would have happened if the Ant had joined the Grasshopper for a chat? (RI.7.3)

Ⓐ The Ant and the Grasshopper would have both starved during the winter.
Ⓑ The Ant and the Grasshopper would have both had plenty of food for the winter.
Ⓒ The Ant and the Grasshopper would never have spent any time together.
Ⓓ The Ant and the Grasshopper would have chatted while they gathered food.

60. Which illustration would best help the reader understand the relationship between the Ant and the Grasshopper?   (RI.7.3)

Ⓐ A text box.
Ⓑ A table and graph.
Ⓒ A Venn diagram.
Ⓓ A picture.

Emily and Jason

Emily and Jason spend every day together. Although both of them would have rather gone home with friends after school, they had no choice but to walk together. Emily could not stand the fact that Jason acted like such a know it all. He was only one year older than she was but he acted like he knew everything. Of course, he never hesitated to tell on her every night at dinner either. Yesterday he complained because she did not clean the sink in the bathroom; last week, he ratted her out for not putting away the laundry. Emily could not wait for next year when she would be able to have the house to herself.

61. What type of relationship do Jason and Emily have?   (RI.7.3)

Ⓐ Jason and Emily are neighbors.
Ⓑ Jason and Emily are classmates.
Ⓒ Jason and Emily walk to school every day.
Ⓓ Jason and Emily are siblings.

62. What incident did Jason mention first?   (RI.7.3)

Ⓐ Emily did not clean the bathroom.
Ⓑ Emily did not put the laundry away.
Ⓒ Emily did not feed the cat.
Ⓓ Emily failed a test at school.

63. What evidence does the author use that allows the reader to infer Jason and Emily's relationship?   (RI.7.3)

Ⓐ They walk home from school together and they eat dinner every night.
Ⓑ They walk home from school together and they argue all the time.
Ⓒ They share a bathroom and have the same chores.
Ⓓ They share a bathroom and she criticizes him often.

Addition

When I was in junior high school, my parents decided to build a new addition onto the back of our house. My sister and I were beyond excited because we thought this would give us a huge game room where we could hang out with all of our friends. Of course, we never expected the new addition to cause so many problems.

First, my parents could not agree on the size of the addition. My Dad wanted it to be a small room with just enough space for a home office; on the other hand, my Mom wanted the addition to large enough to include space for a music and entertainment area. After many discussions back and forth, it was decided that the addition would be a combination of both their wishes. Consequently, the room consisted of a large seating area in the center of the room that faced a television and entertainment center. To the left of the couch and recliners was Dad's computer desk and home office; Mom's grand piano sat to the right.

For the remainder of my time in school, the addition was never empty. Between my sister's and my friends, Mom's music, and Dad's work, we always had something going on in that room. We were so grateful to have the extra space.

64. Which event occurred first in the story?   (RI.7.3)

Ⓐ The author's parents argued over how to configure the space.
Ⓑ The author's parents decided to combine all the ideas into the new addition.
Ⓒ The author's parents could not agree on whether or not to build an addition.
Ⓓ The author's parents decided to build an addition.

65. Which sentence describes the effect of the parent's argument over how to use the room?

(RI.7.3)

Ⓐ First, my parents could not agree on the size of the addition.
Ⓑ My Dad wanted it to be a small room with just enough space for a home office; on the other hand, my Mom wanted the addition to large enough to include space for a music and entertainment area.
Ⓒ We were so grateful to have the extra space.
Ⓓ After many discussions back and forth, it was decided that the addition would be a combination of both their wishes.

Summer Trip

"Juan!" Jacob called out excitedly to his best friend as he ran up to him in the hallway. "You are never going to believe what just happened in Mrs. Smith's class!"

"What, Jake?" Juan was a little unsure of what type of news his friend could have. Jacob had a tendency to get excited about the strangest things.

"She told us we get to go to Washington D.C. and New York City this summer!"

Juan stared at his friend in astonishment. He had always wanted to go to New York City. "No way!" he exclaimed.

"I'm serious! We get to travel as a class, stay in hotels, and visit the Capitol building as well as the White House."

"What about seeing a Broadway play?" Juan asked. "I have always wanted to see The Lion King on stage. My sister saw it when she was in high school and she said it was amazing!"

"Who cares?" Jacob asked with an incredulous look on his face. "We might get to see the President in the White House!"

Juan just shook his head at his friend. "Uh. I don't think he just walks around the White House."
"You never know. But it won't matter if our parents do not agree to let us go."

Jacab knew Juan was right; and more than likely, his parents would not want him to go. They never trusted him to do anything without one of them going as well. Silence filled the air between the two friends for several seconds just before the warning bell sounded. Each was lost in his own thoughts, planning how they could convince their parents to let them go.

"Let's come up with a plan to ask them while we are at lunch." Juan suggested.

Jacob agreed immediately. "That's a great idea! I'll see you then."

66. What suggestion could Juan offer his parents so they agree to let him go on the trip?

(RI.7.3)

Ⓐ Jacob and Juan could room together.
Ⓑ Juan's parents could go as chaperones.
Ⓒ Jacob's brother could go as a chaperone.
Ⓓ He could detail all the wonderful sites the class would be able to explore.

159

67. How did Juan know Jacob might have amazing news?   (RI.7.3)

Ⓐ Jacob ran up to him in the hallway talking excitedly.
Ⓑ Jacob just came from Mrs. Smith's class and she always does cool things.
Ⓒ Jacob enjoys unusual things.
Ⓓ Juan was unsure what kind of news his friend would have.

The Great Round World and What's Going On In It magazine article
Anonymous author

At last beyond any further question Major William McKinley has been elected President of the United States.

The last formality was complied with when, on February 11th, at one o'clock, the **Senate** of the United States, headed by the Vice-President, filed into the **House of Representatives** to count the vote of the Electoral College, cast in the manner described in The Great Round World, No. 13.

As the Senators entered the House of Representatives, all the Congressmen rose, and remained standing while their visitors filed in, two by two.

The little procession was preceded by the officers of the Senate, who carried the ballot boxes.

The work of counting was then commenced by the tellers, and ere long it was officially announced that William McKinley was the choice of the people for President of the United States.

68. What do the bold terms in this selection have in common?   (RI.7.4)

Ⓐ They are all places William McKinley has worked.
Ⓑ They are all parts of the U.S. government.
Ⓒ They are people who work for the President of the U.S.
Ⓓ The Supreme Court

Table of Contents for <u>Flowers of the Farm</u>

69. Based on this table of contents, what can you tell about how this book is organized?

(RI.7.5)

Ⓐ The book is organized by types of flowers.
Ⓑ The book is organized by locations where the flowers can be found.
Ⓒ The book is organized chronologically.
Ⓓ The book is organized by location and type of flower found on the farm.

All about Skunks

Skunks are animals that people both love and hate. To look at them you'd think they are cuddly little critters. They have cute faces that look almost like those of cats and long black and white fur that seems like it would be soft to pet. You might even think, "Flower on the movie <u>Bambi</u> is sweet and Pepe LePew on cartoons doesn't seem so bad. Certainly I could walk up to a skunk and play with it." Yet getting too close to a skunk is a mistake…a big stinky mistake. Though they may look cute and sweet, they hardly smell so! Skunks produce one of the most powerful odors of all animals.

Black and White with a Long Bushy Tail

Skunks are easy to spot because almost all of them look the same. Most of the 12 species or types of skunks have black, bushy fur with a white stripe running down their long tails. There are a few types of skunks that have brown, grey or red fur and one that has what looks like spots instead of a stripe (but is actually an uneven stripe), but for the most part all skunks look pretty much the same. While their appearances may be very much alike, their sizes can be quite different. A skunk can be anywhere from 15.6 inches long to 37 inches long and can weigh between 1.1 pounds and 18 pounds. Skunks are mostly found in Canada, the United States and Mexico though there are a few kinds that live in the Philippines and Indonesia.

Life as a Skunk

For the most part, skunks like to live by themselves. It's not very often that you'll see a group of skunks together. Usually they only travel in groups when the weather is cold. This way they can sleep close together to stay warm.

Skunks are also nocturnal animals. This means that they sleep during the day and are active when it is dark outside. Skunks cannot see very well, but they have excellent senses of smell and hearing. It's not surprising that skunks would rather move around during the night knowing that sight is not their best sense. In fact, most skunks are killed when they happen to wander on to roads and are hit by cars. They cannot see where they are at very well and walk into these dangerous areas.

Skunk Chow

Skunks are omnivores meaning that they eat both plants and animals. They can be found eating nuts, berries, roots, leaves, grasses and even some types of fungi (mushroom-like plants). For animals, they enjoy dining on rodents such as mice and rats, insects, earthworms, frogs, lizards, toads and birds. Sometimes when they are unable to find live animals to eat they become scavengers eating dead animals left behind. When they live close to people's homes, skunks sometimes will even get into trash cans eating garbage.

When skunks eat they do not limit themselves to small meals. They like to "pig out" on whatever food they can find. When there is a large amount of food available skunks get very fat very quickly.

Oooh, that Smell!

What's the first thing you think of when you see a skunk? If you answered "stink" then you're like most people. Many of us connect skunks with their smell. In fact, the name "skunk" comes from the Algonquin Indian word "seganuku" which means "one who squirts". The stinky odor that you smell when skunks are around comes from a liquid that they can spray from two spots near their tails. This "skunk juice" is a mixture of sulfur chemicals. Sulfur is a mineral that smells a lot like rotten eggs which is why skunk spray is so stinky. Watch out if you get any of this juice on you because it is not easy to get off! Skunk spray is very difficult to remove from clothes, skin and hair. Though lots of pet owners swear that you can get a skunk's smell out of a dog's hair by washing him in tomato juice, the best way to remove the scent is by washing the stinky area with a mixture of hydrogen peroxide, baking soda and dish washing soap. This mixture changes the chemicals in the skunk spray so that it no longer stinks.

Not only does skunk juice smell bad, it also stings. A person who happens to get this fluid on his skin will feel like he's been stung by a bee. The burning feeling caused by skunk spray is so strong that if you were to get it in your eyes you might become blind for a short period of time!

Even though it might seem to people who have been sprayed by skunks that the reason for their stinky smell is to annoy us, there is actually a much more important reason why these animals make and squirt their juice. Skunks use their spray to protect themselves from predators (other animals who are trying to attack them). When the average skunk believes that another animal is about to hurt him he will warn it to get away by first stomping his front legs or running forwards and then backwards. Some types of skunks will also hiss or stand up on their front legs. If the predator does not back away, the skunk shoots a cloud of his smelly juice into the air in front of the other animal so that it will have to walk through it to get to him. Skunks are able to spray their juice up to 15 feet. When the predator comes near the cloud of spray he usually is so bothered by the smell that he leaves the skunk alone. The odor from the spray is so powerful that it even keeps bears from attacking skunks!

While skunks are able to use this smelly liquid to protect themselves, they try not to use it too often. They only have enough juice in their bodies at a time to spray 5 or 6 times. It takes a skunk's body at least 2 weeks to make more juice. Luckily, once a predator has been sprayed once by a skunk he doesn't usually forget the event. Many animals will stay away from skunks because they remember their horrible smell. As soon as they see a white stripe on a black body they will run away!

Beyond the Stink

Skunks aren't just stinky animals. They can be very helpful to people. Because they enjoy eating insects and rats sometimes people will purposely put skunks in their yards, on their farms or in their barns to help keep the number of pesky critters down. Some people even enjoy keeping skunks as pets!

http://www.pbs.org/wnet/nature/episodes/is-that-skunk/do-skunks-make-good-pets/4569/

70. If you wanted to find information about how to get the smell of skunk spray out of your dog's fur, which section should you read?   (RI.7.5)

Ⓐ Black and White with a Long Bushy Tail
Ⓑ Life as a Skunk
Ⓒ Skunk Chow
Ⓓ Oooh, that Smell!

71. What does each heading in this selection tell the reader?   (RI.7.5)

Ⓐ An interesting fact about skunks
Ⓑ What the selection is about
Ⓒ The title of another article about skunks
Ⓓ The main idea of the paragraphs below the heading

The Great Barrier Reef

Located off the northeastern coast of Australia is the most complex and diverse eco-system in the world. The Great Barrier Reef is comprised of more than 3,000 individual coral reefs and is home to a plethora of species of plants and animals.

Geology of Great Barrier Reef

Formation of the Great Barrier Reef began millions of years ago. Volcanic activity created what is known as the Coral Sea Basin and a series of raised islands surrounding the basin. As the sea level changed over time so did life living in the basin and on the islands. Over time coral reefs grew, died and were buried under sediment from volcanic eruptions. This layer of rich sediment built up over time forming shelves. The earliest individual coral located on in the raised area now known as the Great Barrier Reef is thought to have formed a half-million years ago. Around 600,000 years ago complete corals began forming in the area and the origin of oldest of those still living today dates back 20,000 years. Sea levels in the area continued to rise until approximately 6,000 years ago. At that point the water level evened out creating the ideal conditions for the formation of a fusion of coral and other plant and animal life. The shallow grounds created by years of volcanic activity and sedimentary build up combined with the warm waters and high levels of sunlight provide the perfect environment for the Great Barrier Reef to form and thrive

Life in the Great Barrier Reef

Within the Great Barrier Reef there are several habitats. Consistent throughout the entire 1,616 mile formation are coral reefs. What we consider a piece of coral is actually a collection of a several individual coral polyps. Each coral is actually a number of polyps. Coral polyps are living creatures that encase themselves in hard, protective shells made of calcium carbonate. These shells band together forming colonies. The colonies together are known as reefs. Within the Great Barrier Reef there are millions of coral featuring a multitude of colors and textures. There are more than 400 species of hard and soft corals living in the Reef.

Housed within the reefs is a vastly diverse collection of animal life, many of which are endangered. Within its waters, the Great Barrier Reef provides homes to 5,000 species of mollusks and 125 species of sharks, stingrays and skates. In addition, there are more than 1,500 species of fish including the colorful clown fish. Thirty species of whales, dolphins and porpoises live in the Great Barrier Reef including humpback whales which use its warm, shallow waters as breeding grounds before journeying to Hawaii to give birth. Six endangered species of marine turtles also use the area to reproduce. The loggerhead turtle, one of the most highly protected endangered species, lives and breeds in the Great Barrier Reef. Over the last 40 years, the number of these turtles has decreased so rapidly that there are only 3% the number of creatures alive today. Housed around this extremely diverse collection of animal life are 2,195 species of plants. Above water 215 species of birds live on the Great Barrier Reef.

Environmental Threats

Because of the diversity, complexity and uniqueness of the eco-system, the Great Barrier Reef was placed under the protection of the Australian federal parks system, was named a World Heritage Site in 1981 and has been called one of the Seven Natural Wonders of the World. Still, life in the Reef is at risk.

Coral Bleaching

One of the greatest threats to the Great Barrier Reef is climate change, also known as global warming. Three times over the last ten years, the water in the seas surrounding the Great Barrier Reef has risen 1 or more degrees Celsius. While this may not seem that significant, any temperature increase threatens the coral reefs. When the water becomes warmer , coral become stressed. This stress causes them to force Zooxanthellae, an algae living in coral shells essential to the sustenance of the coral polyp, out of their shells. Without this algae, the coral is unable to use photosynthesis to form its color which is why the phenomenon is known as "coral bleaching". Once the algae are absent, the coral's white skeleton shows and the coral begins dying, stops reproducing and becomes vulnerable to disease. The Great Barrier Reef experienced episodes of coral bleaching in 1998, 2002 and 2006. Scientists estimate that the 2002 temperature increase caused 60 to 95% of the Reef's coral to become bleached. Because water temperatures are likely to continue to rise, researchers predict that episodes of coral bleaching will continue to occur. Therefore, the Great Barrier Reef Marine Park Authority has formed a response plan aimed at detecting and responding to future occurrences.

Crown of Thorns Starfish

Another natural threat to the Great Barrier Reef is the Crown of Thorns Starfish. This creature which is a naturally occurring species, feeds on coral. While a small number of starfish pose no major threat to the vast collection of coral reefs, when they rapidly multiply, they place the Reef at risk. Eradicating these creature (by forcing them to migrate out of the area) takes anywhere between 1 and 15 years.

Over the last 40 years there have been three major outbreaks of Crown of Thorn Starfish. During those periods large portions of the coral reefs were damaged. These outbreaks combined with episodes of coral bleaching have had dramatic impacts on the coral forming the foundation of the Great Barrier Reef as well as threatening marine and bird species living in the Reef.

Human Impact

Not all of the destruction of the Great Barrier Reef has come from natural sources. Human actions have also negatively impacted the area. Water pollution has threatened life in the Reef. A series of rivers feed the sea where the Reef is located. These rivers have flooded farm lands upstream siphoning large amounts of pesticides used on cattle and sugar cane farms surrounding the rivers. These waters then empty into the seas polluting the waters that the ecosystem.

In addition, land development poses risks to the Great Barrier Reef. Because of its beauty and diversity, the area attracts a huge number of visitors. Though the Reef is protected by the Australian Parks Authority, the tourism industry has built up commercial areas on the lands surrounding the area.

This coastal development threatens the delicate ecosystem adjacent to it.

Beyond this, boats have damaged the Reef. Fishing boats have stripped the area of a number of key species of fish including the Giant Triton. While fishing of certain types of fish has been limited, the boats legitimately fishing in the area pose a potential threat to the entire collection of life located in the Great Barrier Reef. Because the boats carry large amounts of oil necessary for their operation, they always hold the possibility of creating a hazardous situation by spilling the oil into the area's waters.

http://www.reefresilience.org/Toolkit_Coral/C5e2_Government.html

72. How is this selection organized? (RI.7.5)

Ⓐ Using headings
Ⓑ Using subheadings
Ⓒ Using graphics
Ⓓ Using topics

73. If the writer wanted to add the example of people dumping their beach garbage into the reef to the selection, what section would it best fit into? (RI.7.5)

Ⓐ Geology of Great Barrier Reef
Ⓑ Life in the Great Barrier Reef
Ⓒ Coral Bleaching
Ⓓ Human Impact

NOTES

Summer Safety Tips for your Pets

Never leave your pets in a parked car.

In the heat of summer there is no safe amount of time to leave your pet in a parked car. Even if you leave the engine running and the air conditioning on, the temperature inside the vehicle can go up very quickly. According to the Humane Society, on an 85 degree day, the temperature in a car with the windows slightly open can go up to 102 degrees in ten minutes or less. In less than an hour, that temperature can go up to 120 degrees or more! Your pet could suffer permanent organ damage or worse from exposure to high temperatures. If you plan to go somewhere where your pet is not allowed inside, leave him home!

Pets feel humidity too.

Unlike humans, animals don't sweat from pores all over their bodies. Animals pant or breathe rapidly to eliminate heat and moisture from their bodies. If there is a lot of moisture in the air, panting is less effective, and the pet could become overheated and have no way to release that heat. A dehumidifier or air conditioner will remove moisture from the air and make your pet's natural cooling mechanism more effective.

Fans don't help animals very much.

When a human stands in front a fan, the air current rushes over his or her skin and helps evaporate the moisture from sweating. Evaporation helps a human feel cooler. Dogs only sweat from the pads on the bottoms of their feet. Standing in front of a fan doesn't help a dog, since there isn't a large amount of evaporation going on.

Limit exercise on hot days.

Do you feel like running when the temperature is high? Why not? Generally, exercising in extreme heat makes you thirsty and very tired. Too much exercise could lead to heat stroke, a dangerous condition when your body isn't able to cool down. Your pets can suffer the same consequences. When it is extremely hot outside, try to exercise your pet only in the morning or evening when the temperature is cooler, and cut down the amount of time your pet spends running around.
http://www.petfinder.com/dogs/dog-care/leaving-pet-parked-car-deadly/

74. How is this article organized? (RI.7.5)

Ⓐ By subtopic
Ⓑ Chronologically
Ⓒ By order of importance
Ⓓ Alphabetically

169

Advertisement from <u>The Great Round World and What's Going On In It</u> magazine--Anonymous author

Klemm's Practice Relief Maps Advertisement

LIST OF MAPS.

Small size, 9-1/2 x 11	{Plain,	5	cents	each
	{With Waterproofed surface	10	cents	each

Europe, Asia, Africa; North America, South America, East Central States, New England, Middle Atlantic States, South Atlantic States, Palestine, Australia.

Large size, 10 x 15	{Plain,	10	cents	each
	{With Waterproofed surface	15	cents	each

United States, British Isles, Roman Empire, Western Europe, North America, South America, Asia.

(POSTAGE ON SINGLE MAPS, 5 CENTS.)

"I would advise Sunday school teachers to use, in connection with the lessons of 1897, Klemm's Relief Map of the Roman Empire. Every scholar who can draw should have a copy of it. Being blank, it can be beautifully colored: waters, blue; mountains, brown; valleys, green; deserts, yellow; cities marked with pin-holes; and the journeys of Paul can be traced upon it."—Mrs. Wilbur F. Crafts, *President International Union of Primary Sabbath-School Teachers of the United States.*

DESCRIPTION OF THE MAPS.

These maps are made in two forms, both with beautifully executed relief (embossed)—the cheaper ones of plain stiff paper similar to drawing paper (these are to be substituted for and used as outline map blanks), the others covered with a durable waterproof surface, that can be quickly cleaned with a damp sponge, adapted to receive a succession of markings and cleansings. Oceans, lakes, and rivers, as well as land, appear in the same color, white, so as to facilitate the use of the map as a *geographical slate.*

WILLIAM BEVERLEY HARISON
3 & 5 W. 18th St. • • • New York City

75. What strategy does the author of this advertisement use to try to convince readers his point of view is shared by others?   (RI.7.6)

Ⓐ He describes the maps in detail.
Ⓑ He uses a testimonial from someone who uses the maps.
Ⓒ He lists the costs of the maps at the beginning of the ad.
Ⓓ He lists all the different types of maps that can be purchased from Klemm's.

PASSAGE A:

When I was in the fourth grade no one liked me because my brother was arrested and that made everyone think that I might do something illegal, too. It hurt my feelings to have to sit through school every day and not talk to anyone. When it was time to work in groups I would have to sit with a group of kids that I knew hated me. Sometimes they would say something mean or move a chair away when it looked like I might sit with them. It was worse during lunch and on the bus when kids would yell things about my brother and ask me if I visited him in prison. After a while I didn't want to go to school anymore and I pretended to be sick every day so I could stay home. Telling my parents and my teachers didn't change anything. After a while my parents decided to let me change schools. The first year at my new school was bad because I didn't know anyone and was afraid to talk to people because of everything that happened at the old school. After a while I made a few friends and I started to feel better about talking to people. Now I have a few friends and I don't feel like people are bullying me anymore.

PASSAGE B:

According to Dr. Norman Anderson, CEO of the American Psychological Association, bullying is any kind of aggressive behavior in which someone intentionally tries to harm or cause discomfort to another person. Bullying can be in the form of physical contact, but is just as frequently demonstrated in cruel remarks, intentional exclusion of the victim, or in recent years, cyber bullying, in which the aggressor lashes out to the victim via email, social networking, or text messaging.

There is no single, identifiable cause of bullying. Bullying often occurs as a result of influences from peer groups, family groups, community, or even the media. It is, therefore, important to engage all of these groups if any anti-bullying effort is to be successful.

For many years, the primary means employed by schools to deal with student to student bullying has been to punish the aggressor. Research has shown that disciplinary consequences alone will not significantly curb bullying in academic settings. Faculty and administrators must be trained to identify early warning signs that students are either bullies or being bullied, and onlookers, students who are not bullies themselves, but do nothing to inhibit bullying they witness, must be empowered with interpersonal skills training to help them intervene when they witness bullying within their peer groups.

76. **According the author of Passage B, what strategy would most likely have helped the author of Passage A?**   (RI.7.9)

    Ⓐ Disciplinary consequences for the bullies
    Ⓑ Changing schools
    Ⓒ Training "onlookers" to intervene when they witness bullying
    Ⓓ Counseling for the bullying victim

77. **What information from Passage B best explains this line from Passage A:**
Telling my parents and my teachers didn't change anything.   (RI.7.9)

    Ⓐ Research has shown that disciplinary consequences alone will not significantly curb bullying in academic settings.
    Ⓑ Bullying often occurs as a result of influences from peer groups, family groups, community, or even the media.
    Ⓒ Bullying can be in the form of physical contact, but is just as frequently demonstrated in cruel remarks, intentional exclusion of the victim, or in recent years, cyber bullying, in which the aggressor lashes out to the victim via email, social networking, or text messaging.
    Ⓓ For many years, the primary means employed by schools to deal with student to student bullying has been to punish the aggressor.

78. **Which passage was most likely written by a middle school student?**   (RI.7.9)

    Ⓐ Passage A
    Ⓑ Passage B
    Ⓒ Both passages
    Ⓓ There is not enough information to determine the authors.

79. Which passage explains what is meant by bullying?   (RI.7.9)

Ⓐ Passage A
Ⓑ Passage B
Ⓒ Both passages
Ⓓ Neither passage

80. Which form of bullying described in Passage B was experienced by the author of Passage A?   (RI.7.9)

Ⓐ Physical contact
Ⓑ Intentional exclusion
Ⓒ Bullying by way of social media
Ⓓ Cyber-bullying

Success

One should guard against preaching to young people success in the customary form as the main aim in life. The most important motive for work in school and in life is pleasure in work, pleasure it is result, and the knowledge of the value of the result to the community.
- Albert Einstein

The way to learn to do things is to do things. The way to learn a trade is to work at it. Success teaches how to succeed. Begin with the determination to succeed, and the work is half-done already.
- Henry Ford

"What Constitutes Success"
By Bessie Stanley (1905)

He has achieved success who has lived well,
laughed often and loved much;
who has gained the respect of intelligent men
and the love of little children;
who has filled his niche and accomplished his task;
who has left the world better than he found it,
whether by an improved poppy, a perfect poem, or a rescued soul;
who has never lacked appreciation of earth's beauty
or failed to express it;
who has always looked for the best in others

and given them the best he had;
whose life was an inspiration;
whose memory a benediction.

81. Which of the other two authors likely shared Einstein's idea of what constitutes success?

(RI.7.9)

Ⓐ Henry Ford
Ⓑ Bessie Stanley
Ⓒ Both authors.
Ⓓ Neither author.

82. Which of the authors most likely subscribed to what Einstein referred to as "success in the customary form?"

(RI.7.9)

Ⓐ Albert Einstein
Ⓑ Bessie Stanley
Ⓒ Henry Ford
Ⓓ None of the authors.

Steve Jobs, the CEO of Apple Computer, once said, "Being the richest man in the cemetery doesn't matter to me...Going to bed at night saying I've done something wonderful...that's what matters to me."

83. Which of the expressions about success above most closely align with Jobs' idea?

(RI.7.9)

Ⓐ Albert Einstein
Ⓑ Henry Ford
Ⓒ Bessie Stanley
Ⓓ Both B and C.

84. Which of the authors above aligns themselves with the desire to succeed through industrial work for the common man?

Ⓐ Albert Einstein
Ⓑ Henry Ford
Ⓒ Bessie Stanley
Ⓓ Both Ford and Einstein

85. Which of the authors above would most strongly disagree with Ford's interpretation of success?   (RI.7.9)

Ⓐ Albert Einstein
Ⓑ Steve Jobs
Ⓒ Bessie Stanley
Ⓓ None of the above.

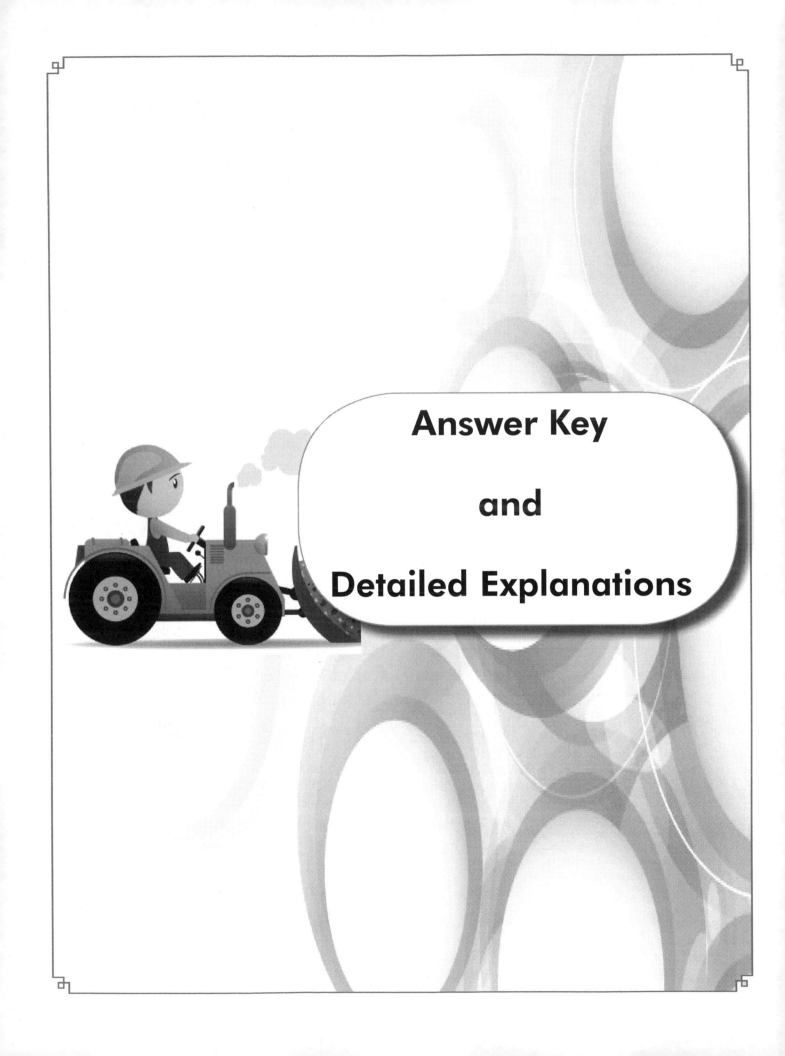

Answer Key

and

Detailed Explanations

Question No.	Answer	Detailed Explanations	CCSS
1	C	Answer choice three is correct. In the last few lines of the poem tells the reader that the pig had a ring on the end of his nose, and that he is willing to sell it for a shilling (type of money).	RL.7.1
2	A	Answer choice one is correct. The captain came back, but he was in a wheelchair. Also, he said he had a leg that was nearly "blown off." These facts explain why he came back home.	RL.7.1
3	C	Answer choice three is the best answer. The poem discusses how feeling sorry for oneself is not good because everyone has their problems. And often, they are worse than yours.	RL.7.2
4	C	Answer one is incorrect because the boy was not disobedient. He did as his father asked. Answer two is incorrect because there was no mention of anyone going to Heaven, just a new/different life. Answer three is the best choice because the boy respected and obeyed his father, when he did not want to. However, the end result is not what the father had hoped for. The story tells about acquiring a spirit, but it does not specifically mention dying.	RL.7.2
5	A	Answer one is the best choice. The young man felt he needed to be excused from the fast, but his father would not listen to his son. The father could have still asked his son to remain with his fast, after hearing his son's concerns. But, the father would not even hear what his son had to say. Answer two is incorrect because the strictness of the father was NOT effective to the father's hopes. Answer choice three is not the best answer because the word "always" is used. Any choice that uses "always," or other absolutes are usually not good answer choices. Answer choice four is incorrect because the boy did not take his father for granted, or take advantage of him. This is not a reasonable theme of this story.	RL.7.2

177

Question No.	Answer	Detailed Explanations	CCSS
6	B	Answer choice one is not the best answer. Yes, people should watch out for falling objects, but that is not the point of this poem. Answer choice two is the best answer choice. The acorn, although small, had a big impact in this story. Answer choice three is not the best answer because Mother Nature is not questioned in the passage. The fourth answer choice is not the best choice because not EVERY seed becomes a beautiful plant. Some don't grow at all, others sprout into weeds. Try to avoid answer choices that use absolutes such as "always" or "every."	RL.7.2
7	C	Answer choice three is the best answer. The fact that lumber had to be brought in on a wagon (horse drawn) tells the reader that this was written before the motor vehicle was invented.	RL.7.3
8	C	Answer choice three is the best answer. The words to describe their habitats are fun and non-sensical (Sofsky-Popsky and Pipple Popple). This helps sets the tone of silly. There is no indication of greed or really of constant hunger. And whether the animals are diverse or not does not answer the question about tone.	RL.7.4
9	B	Answer choice two is correct. The reader knows the author is repulsed because of the word choice. The author uses words that are not flattering to the woman. The descriptions of her body frame in the coat as well as the negative comment about the length of her skirt tell the reader that she is not attractive (the opposite of repulse). Also, the author mentions the bad teeth. This does not paint a pretty picture for the reader.	RL.7.4
10	A	Answer choice one is the best choice. The author is comparing the sisters to little birds in a nest (metaphor). The author is trying to illustrate how siblings pick on one another by comparing them to birds in a nest who literally peck their siblings.	RL.7.4
11	A	Answer choice one is the correct answer. Jo wants to buy a book, and the author calling her a "bookworm" helps indicate this.	RL.7.4
12	A	Answer choice one is the best answer. The author describes the Martians as organized and thoughtful. So, the tone is one of admiration.	RL.7.4

Question No.	Answer	Detailed Explanations	CCSS
13	A	Answer choice one is the correct answer.	RL.7.4
14	A	Answer choice one is the best answer. If a person does not have dreams there is no reason to work hard to achieve other things.	RL.7.4
15	A	Part of the definition of a villanelle is that it have two rhyming patterns. This poem has two rhyming patterns so answer choice number one is the answer to select.	RL.7.5
16	D	In poetry repetition is used to stress an idea, sound or feeling. The word me is not repeated, so answer choice number four is the best answer.	RL.7.5
17	D	The correct answer is answer choice four. The way this poem is structured in rhyme helps lead the reader from one stanza to the next. This helps with pacing and feeling connected.	RL.7.5
18	C	Answer choice number three is the best answer. When the author states she got the story "bit by bit" from various people, and that it was slightly different each time, she is hinting that she has pieced the story together, and the accuracy is not necessarily the way it actually happened.	RL.7.5
19	B	Answer choice two is the best answer. If the author had explained how she learned of the story, it would help the reader analyze the accuracy of the story and the person telling the story. It would give the story as told more credit.	RL.7.5
20	A	Answer choice number one is the best answer. The prologue is written to rhyme, like a poem. The remaining portion of the passage is written in the format of a play (prose=anything not poetic).	RL.7.5
21	D	Answer four is the correct answer. Because the first two lines rhyme with one another, and then each pair of lines after that rhyme, the rhyme scheme is aa, bb, cc, dd.	RL.7.5
22	C	Answer choice three is the best choice. The man in this poem is traveling late at night and he stops for seemingly no reason. A horse that is accustomed to traveling the same paths/roads would realize something was out of the ordinary. His shaking of bells would be an indication of the horse "asking" why they are stopped.	RL.7.5

Question No.	Answer	Detailed Explanations	CCSS
23	B	The second choice is the correct answer. When analyzing a poem each sound is assigned a letter. Any time that sound appears it is assigned the same letter. When a new sound presents itself, the next letter in the alphabet is assigned. The scheme can be simple, aabb, or very complex, aaba,bbcd etc.	RL.7.5
24	D	Answer choice four is the correct answer. This line indicates that the author hopes to be telling this story a long time from now.	RL.7.5
25	A	Answer choice one is the correct answer. The passage explains that the swindlers (dishonest people) told the Emperor that if a person was wise, and worthy of their job/status, they would be able to see the fabric/costumes. But, the men never intended to make any clothes. No one was willing to admit that they saw no clothes because they did not want to appear to be unworthy. It took a child, who did not know to hide what he saw, to point out the obvious. The remaining three answers describe the swindlers (2 and 3) and what an official thought upon seeing the "clothes." They do not answer the question: **Why** did the Emperor agree to hire the men (swindlers).	RL.7.6
26	A	Answer choice one is the best answer. The king is insecure about himself and that is why he hired the swindlers. He only cares about looks and he wanted a "trick" to help him with his work/people. The minister would be considered wise and trustworthy, so if he could not see the fabric, he would be out of a job. Not seeing the fabric made him feel as though maybe he really wasn't good enough for the job. Choice two is incorrect because the minister never indicated he wanted to fool the public. Choice three is incorrect because only the Emperor was worried about clothes. And answer four is incorrect. The Emperor thought the minister could see things not visible. The Emperor never claimed to.	RL.7.6

Question No.	Answer	Detailed Explanations	CCSS
27	B	Answer choice two is the best answer. The passage states that the Emperor knows he has no clothes on. He continues though because he does not want to admit he was wrong, and that he was tricked by the swindlers. Answer choice one is incorrect because he did believe him, he knew it to be true. Answer choices two and three are incorrect because no one can see what is not there, and he can't show off nothing.	RL.7.6
28	A	Answer choice one is the correct answer. The beginning of the passage Huck mentions his father used to hit him. Then, when he sees his father, he realizes he should not be afraid of him anymore. Answer choice two is incorrect because his father WANTS him to STOP going to school. The remaining answer choices deal with his friends. His father is only interested in Huck not being "better than his dad" and any money Huck might have on him.	RL.7.6
29	C	Answer choice three is the correct answer. First, Huck's father slaps the book from Buck's hands, but then he tells him to stay away from the school. Answer choice four is incorrect because he does not ask to learn to read. He seems proud that neither he nor Huck's mom could read or write. Answer choice one is incorrect because Huck's father is NOT proud of him. He does demand Huck give him money, but he is not proud. Answer choice two is partially correct, but not the best answer. Huck's father does hit the book from his hand, but the question asked is what does Huck's father ask/tell him to do. Not what does Huck's dad do.	RL.7.6
30	B	Answer choice two is the best answer. His attitude towards them is one of shame. They don't come outside at all, and he finds that odd. Answer choice three is incorrect because he is allowed inside (Judge's feet), and answer four is not reasonable. No dogs tease him.	RL.7.6

Question No.	Answer	Detailed Explanations	CCSS
31	C	Answer choice three is the correct answer. He did not want to be a house dog. He does not respect those dogs who do nothing dog-like. He does not want to be a kennel dog because those dogs are working dogs. He enjoys being part of the family, being around the family, and he is proud of his place. He is trusted with being involved/caring for the family.	RL.7.6
32	C	Answer choice three is correct. Buck feels that it is strange that they rarely put nose out of doors (go outside) or put their feet to the ground (someone holds/carries them all the time). The three remaining answers may be true, but they do not hint at Buck's opinions of the two inside dogs.	RL.7.6
33	B	Answer choice two is the correct answer. After a long, long trip he is relaxing and getting well. He mentions being surprised that the other dogs are not jealous. This indicates being relieved that he does not have to worry about dog fights or any other issues with jealousy.	RL.7.6
34	D	The last answer choice is the answer choice that does NOT describe Buck. He is honorable in his actions (the Jude's), he is persistent (went for long walks and kept others company) and he is grateful (for Thornton and Skeet). Nothing in these passages indicate aggression.	RL.7.6
35	C	Answer choice three is the best answer. All answers might be correct depending on who holds the opinion, but the author's opinion in this poem is that it is not good for siblings to argue. So, the answer choice three is not in agreement with the author's view.	RL.7.7
36	A	Answer choice one is the correct answer. The ingredients are non-sensical, and the directions are silly. It is not a true recipe, as nothing would be produced by completing the steps.	RL.7.7
37	C	Answer choice three is the correct answer. This poem says that a bird will give the message of love. Modern valentine cards and poems usually mention hearts and candy. Answers one and two are characteristics of modern valentines. Answer choice four is not applicable to the question. There is a difference.	RL.7.7
38	B	Answer choice two is the best answer. The question asks what the poem and the holiday have in common. Both have fireworks.	RL.7.7

Question No.	Answer	Detailed Explanations	CCSS
39	A	The first answer choice is the best choice. The first line of the second stanza tells the reader what Revere was planning to do.	RL.7.9
40	B	Answer choice two. The first line of the second paragraph states why Revere was riding.	RL.7.9
41	B	Answer choice two is the best choice. The poem and the passage cover the same historical event. The poem is more entertaining and gives the same information, but leaves out Revere's arrest.	RL.7.9
42	A	Answer choice one is the best choice. Left without a horse is not in the poem, and it would not be because the poem is intended to celebrate the heroics of Revere.	RL.7.9
43	D	The fourth answer choice is the correct one. Dawes and Revere were together almost the entire ride.	RL.7.9
44	D	Answer choice four is the best choice. Factual information from survivors reported that the band played until the very last, but does not explain why.	RL.7.9
45	C	The last stanza of the poem expresses the commitment the band had to helping in any way they could. Answer choice number three is the best answer.	RL.7.9
46	B	Answer choice two is the best choice. The band played on and on trying to boost the spirits of those on the deck of the boat.	RL.7.9
47	C	Answer choice three is the best answer. The poem, in particular, mentions why the band is needed by explaining different situations of chaos.	RL.7.9
48	C	Answer choice three is the correct answer. Both women saw the boat go down, one even mentioned nearly being sucked under by the ship, so they would know what happened at the last minute.	RL.7.9
49	A	Answer choice one is correct. The other choices explain what the skin does, but none come closer than choice one to explaining WHY it is being developed.	RI.7.1
50	C	Answer choice three is correct. It explains that dogs can smell low blood sugar, so the reader can infer that's what helps diabetic patients. The other choices talk about the training research, and diabetics in general.	RI.7.1

Question No.	Answer	Detailed Explanations	CCSS
51	A	Answer choice one is correct. The researcher wants to reproduce the sensitivity in a way that will help patients. Dogs already have the sensitivity, so choices two and three are not correct, and choice four, while plausible, doesn't seem very useful.	RI.7.1
52	A	Answer choice one is correct. The sentence explains that training dogs is slow and expensive, so the reader can infer that by reproducing the sensitivity, they can save money and time, making it easier to help more people.	RI.7.1
53	A	Answer choice one is correct. Rule three discusses what happens if you are tardy. Other choices relate to being prepared and knowing what to do when class starts or if you miss class.	RI.7.1
54	A	Answer choice one is correct. The other choices talk about the effects and aftermath of his decision.	RI.7.1
55	B	Answer choice two is correct. Booth was an actor, so that likely helped him gain access to the theatre. The other choices do not help answer the question.	RI.7.1
56	A	Answer choice one is the best answer. Lincoln was concerned that the country might stay divided even after the war ended. He was attempting to get people to understand that if the country did not come back together as one nation that all the men who died in the Civil War would have died for nothing. He believes to honor the dead, the country should stay as one.	RI.7.2
57	A	Answer choice one is the best answer. The other answer choices are related to the passage, except for three, but they are not the BEST answers. The best choice indicates that Woo is very good at action scenes and loves to do them. Answer choice three is not at all reasonable for this passage.	RI.7.2
58	C	Answer choice number three is the best answer. The relationship is causal, or an "acquaintance" in nature. There is nothing about being related, and they are not enemies, no anger exists. Also, they are not best friends, or the question would not need to be asked. The BEST answer is the third, They know one another, but they don't fully "get" each other.	RI.7.3

Question No.	Answer	Detailed Explanations	CCSS
59	A	The best answer choice is the first one. The ant was hard at work preparing for the future, and had he stopped to visit with the grasshopper he would have not been prepared.	RI.7.3
60	C	Answer choice three is the best answer. The question asks about a relationship between two things (grasshopper and ant). A Venn diagram is strategy used to compare two different items. A picture illustrates, not necessarily compares. A graph or table are used for numbers or value data. A text box could be used for words and description, but not the BEST way to compare.	RI.7.3
61	D	The best answer choice is the last one. The passage explains a relationship. They live together. One of them is older than the other and is bossy. The first two answers cannot be correct because they indicate that Emily and Jason do not live together. The passage states that they do live together. The third answer choice is not mentioned. They walk home from school, but there is nothing to indicate they walk together in the morning.	RI.7.3
62	B	Answer choice number two is the best choice. If the reader wrote the events in order as they occurred in time, they could see that the laundry incident happened last week, prior to other events.	RI.7.3
63	A	Answer choice number one is the best answer choice. The other options are possible, but based on the passage, the first answer choice is the BEST. There is no mention of having the same chores, criticizing him, or sharing a bathroom.	RI.7.3
64	D	Answer choice four is the best answer. This is found in the first paragraph, stated clearly.	RI.7.3
65	D	Answer choice number four is the best choice. The question asks the reader the consequence of the parents disagreement. It is a result of the disagreement.	RI.7.3
66	B	Answer choice number two is the best answer. The passage mentions that the parents usually wanted to be with their children on trips like such as this. The other answer choices aren't reasonable in helping ease the parents' concerns. So, the best answer is getting their parents to go as chaperones.	RI.7.3

Question No.	Answer	Detailed Explanations	CCSS
67	A	Answer choice one is the best one. Talking excitedly would indicate that someone had something unusual or good to share.	RI.7.3
68	B	Answer choice two is the best answer. This passage is about counting the votes to elect President McKinley. The process is described and includes the Senate and the House of Representatives. These are parts of the U. S. Government.	RI.7.4
69	D	Answer choice four is the correct answer. The title of the book tells the reader the subject of the book. Each chapter title is a <u>place</u> on the <u>farm</u> where <u>specific flowers</u> would grow. Answers one and two are correct, but four is the most correct. Answer three does not make sense for this question.	
70	D	Answer choice four is the correct answer. This section discusses the odor that skunks' spray causes. It also discusses how to alleviate the smell by giving suggestions on what to use to bathe the affected person/animal. None of the remaining three answers discuss removing the smell from a person or animal.	
71	D	Answer choice four is the best answer. Answer choice one is correct, but not a complete answer. Answer choice two is also correct, but not as good answer as choice number four. Answer choice three is not correct for this passage. Therefore, answer choice four is the best answer because it is the most complete.	
72	A	Answer choice one is the correct answer. The title is at the top of the passage, but sections are labeled with headings to help the reader know what the main topic of the paragraph(s) will be. Graphics are not used, topics are, but the headings are the main way the reader knows the topics. Subheadings are not used.	
73	D	Answer choice four is the correct answer. Humans would dump garbage, and so this is the heading that makes the most sense.	
74	A	Answer choice one is the correct answer. The topic of the article is at the beginning. Each section is about a different tip or concern. This is a sub-topical organization.	

Question No.	Answer	Detailed Explanations	CCSS
75	B	Answer choice two is the correct answer. A testimonial is a technique of advertising where someone who has used the product shares their experiences (positive). This is intended to encourage others to use/buy the product as well.	
76	C	Answer choice number three is the correct selection. If someone had been able to intervene, it would have helped the victim in the first passage. The other three answers are good answers in general, but the third answer best fits the situation of the boy in passage A.	
77	A	Answer choice one is the correct answer. The first passage tells an incident, the second passage is informational. They are both about bullying, but from a different genre.	
78	A	Answer choice one is correct. The first passage tells of about a young man who was a victim of bullying. The second passage is informational and contains information, that mostly adults would know. So, the first answer choice is the correct one.	
79	C	Answer choice three is correct. Both passages explain bullying.	
80	B	Answer choice two is correct. All three of the other answers are forms of bullying, but not the experience of the victim in the first passage.	
81	B	Answer choice two is the best answer. Einstein was someone who was not always thinking and behaving "normal." His ideas were very unusual for his time, so the free thinking of Stanley is more aligned with the scientist.	
82	C	Answer choice three is the correct answer. Ford was a creative person, but his ideas were more business minded. So, his ideas were more "customary" or normal.	
83	D	Both Einstein and Stanley wanted a better world.	
84	B	Answer choice number two is the correct answer. Ford was responsible for the assembly line, something that most people could do, and it helped to change the way industry ran in America. But, his ideas and attitudes were more for the regular person, whereas the others were very broad and difficult for many people to grasp.	
85	C	Answer choice three is correct. Stanley gives more of an air of societal success, which in itself is more likely to be criticized.	

NOTES

Common Core Standards Cross-reference Table

CCSS	Standard Description	Page No./ Question No.
RL.7.1	Cite several pieces of textual evidence to support analysis of what the text says explicitly as well as inferences drawn from the text.	p8/1; p9/2; p10/1; p11/2; p13/1; p14/1 to 3; p15/1 to 3; p16/4; p17/1, 2; p18/3; p21/1; p26/1; p29/1; p106/1; p108/2
RL.7.2	Determine a theme or central idea of a text and analyze its development over the course of the text; provide an objective summary of the text.	p11/3 to 5; p18/4; p26/2, 3; p33/1, 2; p34/1; p36/1, 2; p40/1; p41/1; p42/2; p44/1; p111/4 to 6
RL.7.3	Analyze how particular elements of a story or drama interact (e.g., how setting shapes the characters or plot).	p9/3 to 5; p11/6; p12/7 to 9; p13/2, 3; p18/5, 6; p21/2, 3; p22/4, 5; p26/4, 5; p29/2 to 5; p30/6; p33/3; p34/2; p36/3; p37/4; p40/2; p42/3; p44/2; p45/1; p108/4; p113/7
RL.7.4	Determine the meaning of words and phrases as they are used in a text, including figurative and connotative meanings; analyze the impact of rhymes and other repetitions of sounds (e.g., alliteration) on a specific verse or stanza of a poem or section of a story or drama.	p37/5; p41/1, 2; p115/8; p116/9; p119/10 to13; p120/14
RL.7.5	Analyze how a drama's or poem's form or structure (e.g., soliloquy, sonnet) contributes to its meaning.	p121/15 to 17; p122/18, 19; p126/20; p127/21, 22; p128/23; p129/24
RL.7.6	Analyze how an author develops and contrasts the points of view of different characters or narrators in a text.	p133/25 to 27; p136/28; p137/29, 30; p138/31 to 34
RL.7.7	Compare and contrast a written story, drama, or poem to its audio, filmed, staged, or multimedia version, analyzing the effects of techniques unique to each medium (e.g., lighting, sound, color, or camera focus and angles in a film).	p37/6; p40/3; p46/2, 3; p48/3; p139/35; p140/36; p141/37, 38
RL.7.9	Compare and contrast a fictional portrayal of a time, place, or character and a historical account of the same period as a means of understanding how authors of fiction use or alter history.	p145/39 to 42; p146/43; p148/44 to 46; p149/47, 48
RI.7.1	Cite several pieces of textual evidence to support analysis of what the text says explicitly as well as inferences drawn from the text.	p49/1; p51/1, 2; p55/1; p149/49; p150/50, 51; p151/52, 53; p152/54, 55

CCSS	Standard Description	Page No./ Question No.
RI.7.2	Determine two or more central ideas in a text and analyze their development over the course of the text; provide an objective summary of the text.	p27/6; p49/2; p56/1; p58/1; p61/1; p62/1; p67/1; p153/56; p154/57
RI.7.3	Analyze the interactions between individuals, events, and ideas in a text (e.g., how ideas influence individuals or events, or how individuals influence ideas or events).	p156/58 to 60; p157/61 to 63; p158/64, 65; p159/66; p160/67
RI.7.4	Determine the meaning of words and phrases as they are used in a text, including figurative, connotative, and technical meanings; analyze the impact of a specific word choice on meaning and tone.	p27/7; p49/3; p52/3, 4; p61/2; p62/2; p69/1; p70/1; p72/1; p160/68
RI.7.5	Analyze the structure an author uses to organize a text, including how the major sections contribute to the whole and to the development of the ideas.	p67/2; p73/1; p77/1; p78/1; p161/69; p164/70, 71; p167/72, 73; p169/74
RI.7.6	Determine an author's point of view or purpose in a text and analyze how the author distinguishes his or her position from that of others.	p50/4; p61/3; p63/3; p67/3; p69/2; p71/2; p72/2; p79/2; p80/1; p171/75
RI.7.7	Compare and contrast a text to an audio, video, or multimedia version of the text, analyzing each medium's portrayal of the subject (e.g., how the delivery of a speech affects the impact of the words).	p50/5; p55/2 to 4; p57/2 to 4; p59/2 to 4
RI.7.8	Trace and evaluate the argument and specific claims in a text, assessing whether the reasoning is sound and the evidence is relevant and sufficient to support the claims.	p55/5; p59/5; p61/4; p63/4; p71/3; p77/2; p79/3; p80/2
RI.7.9	Analyze how two or more authors writing about the same topic shape their presentations of key information by emphasizing different evidence or advancing different interpretations of facts.	p172/76 to 78; p173/79, 80; p174/81 to 84; p175/85

Online Resources

CCSS	URL	QR Code
RL.7.1	http://lumoslearning.com/a/15363	
RL.7.1	http://lumoslearning.com/a/15364	
RL.7.2	http://lumoslearning.com/a/15365	
RL.7.2	http://lumoslearning.com/a/15366	
RL.7.3	http://lumoslearning.com/a/15367	

CCSS	URL	QR Code
RL.7.3	http://lumoslearning.com/a/15368	
RL.7.3	http://lumoslearning.com/a/15369	
RL.7.4	http://lumoslearning.com/a/15370	
RL.7.5	http://lumoslearning.com/a/15371	
RL.7.6	http://lumoslearning.com/a/15372	

CCSS	URL	QR Code
RL.7.7	http://lumoslearning.com/a/15375	
RL.7.9	http://lumoslearning.com/a/15373	
RI.7.1	http://lumoslearning.com/a/15376	
RI.7.2	http://lumoslearning.com/a/15377	
RI.7.3	http://lumoslearning.com/a/15378	

CCSS	URL	QR Code
RI.7.4	http://lumoslearning.com/a/15379	
RI.7.5	http://lumoslearning.com/a/15380	
RI.7.6	http://lumoslearning.com/a/15381	
RI.7.7	http://lumoslearning.com/a/15382	
RI.7.8	http://lumoslearning.com/a/15384	

CCSS	URL	QR Code
RI.7.9	http://lumoslearning.com/a/15383	

Other Books in SkillBuilder Series

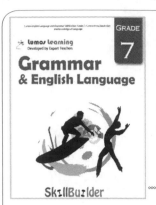

English Language and Grammar SkillBuilder

- Conventions
- Vocabulary
- Knowledge of Language

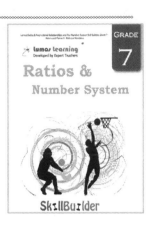

Ratios & Proportional Relationships and The Number System SkillBuilder

- Unit Rates
- Measurement
- Division of Whole Numbers

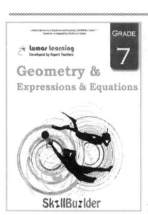

Expressions & Equations and Geometry SkillBuilder

- Evaluating Expressions
- Surface Area
- Volume

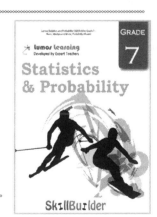

Statistics and Probability SkillBuilder

- Distribution
- Graphs
- Charts

http://lumoslearning.com/a/sbtb

Made in the USA
San Bernardino, CA
01 June 2018